McALEESE'S FIGHTING MANUAL

ALSO BY PETER McALEESE

No Mean Soldier

McALEESE's
FIGHTING MANUAL

PETER McALEESE AND JOHN AVERY

ORION

Copyright © Peter McAleese and John Avery 1998

All rights reserved

The right of Peter McAleese and John Avery to be identified
as the authors of this work has been asserted by them in
accordance with the Copyright, Designs and Patents Act 1988.

First published in 1998 by Orion
An imprint of Orion Books Ltd
Orion House, 5 Upper St Martin's Lane, London WC2H 9EA

A CIP catalogue record for this book is available
from the British Library

ISBN 0 75280 063 9

Printed in Great Britain by
Butler & Tanner Ltd, Frome and London

Contents

vi Introduction

PART 1: TACTICS
3   Prepare for battle
13   Patrols
38   Ambushes
57   Defensive battle
69   Nuclear, biological and chemical warfare

PART 2: THEATRES OF WAR
75   Fighting in the desert
80   Fighting in the jungle
86   Fighting in the bush
96   Fighting in Arctic conditions
105 Fighting in cities
121 Fighting in forests and woods
124 Fighting at night

PART 3: COMBAT SURVIVAL
133 Battlefield first aid
143 Escape and evasion
148 Prisoners of war
155 Survival skills

PART 4: MARKSMANSHIP
161 Range safety
162 Principles of marksmanship
169 Battle shooting

IMPORTANT

All military or survival training involves risk of injury and must be carried out with care. Expert guidance must be sought and equipment checked for reliability before any such activity described in this book is undertaken. The authors and publishers cannot accept responsibility for any injury, death, loss or damage which may result from carrying out activities described in this book.

Introduction

Soldiering is in my blood. In my autobiography, *No Mean Soldier*, I described my military career from the Parachute Regiment to the SAS, from the Angolan War to soldiering with the Rhodesian SAS and South African Defence Force. I've survived over a hundred contacts and I can say, without being boastful, that I was one of the best. Now I'm putting down on paper the military lessons I've learned along the way.

Nobody's going to become a great soldier simply by reading this book; on the other hand, nobody knows it all. Whether you are in the cadets, TA or have just signed on for another nine years, there's enough in here to get you thinking. And if you are not in the forces, but want to know how things are done, this is as close as you can get without getting your feet wet.

The SAS regimental journal said of *No Mean Soldier*, 'McAleese is scathing of the modern SAS'. Whoever wrote that probably won't like this book either, because I am going to tell a few home truths. But let's get one thing straight: I'm not being critical for the sake of it. If I seem too critical of the special forces, it's because that's where I've spent most of my time. And the intense publicity given to the SAS from the storming of the Iranian Embassy to the Falklands and the Gulf War have given the regiment enormous influence over the rest of the army. Everyone wants to do it 'like the SAS'. So we must look very carefully at what exactly the special forces are doing; if we take everything they do uncritically, we could make some terrible errors. Special forces are not perfect; the infamous Bravo 20 patrol demonstrated that. I know I'm right. I fought in Africa and we had next to no logistical support. To fly in an SAS squadron these days you're talking about a jumbo jet for the guys and another for all their kit. What's happened to the days when you carried everything in your rucksacks? I still believe in the boys. I believe that from the bottom of my heart. The material is there, it's just what's being done with it.

The prominence of the special forces is leading to another problem: over-specialisation. There's too much jargon, and too much posing. They don't fight in the jungle, they go 'patrolling green'. Anti-terrorist work is 'black soldiering'.

Whatever's next? Beige soldiering for desert warfare? White soldiering for Arctic warfare? Self-conscious élitism has two dangerous consequences. Firstly, you lose your ability to question yourself and your methods, leading to over-confidence and the catalogue of errors that made the Bravo 20 disaster. Secondly, it creates a divide between the special forces and the soldiers of all other regiments. We already have a situation in Northern Ireland where guys in infantry regiments do the groundwork, put in the hours in the OP, only to have the actual ambush of the terrorists conducted by a team of spooks brought in from outside. By all means have the special forces as something for guys to aspire to, but don't create an 'us and them' situation that insults the professionalism of the rest of the army.

Old soldiers have been telling young recruits how much harder it was in their day since Roman times. But I really am concerned that the British Army is losing it, that 'the beast' is gone. Too many people think that modern gadgets can do the work for them, that they don't need to know how to navigate properly because they have global positioning systems. Others seem to believe that with enough Gore-tex and similar special clothing they can go into the field and never get wet or cold. This concern with physical comfort has been elevated into a fine theory called the comfort zone the longer you can keep a guy comfortable, the longer his military efficiency remains at its peak. Fine. I've slept in a trench full of water. I never had Gore-tex kit. I got trench foot once on an escape and evasion exercise, and I never want to experience that again. But are we getting to the stage that unless we have the kit, the personal comfort gear, we're not going to go to war? I hope not, because there's a lot of guys out there who don't mind being uncomfortable, who are ready to take us on.

The obsession with personal comfort is leading to soldiers carrying too much kit. I've seen guys lugging around the most monstrous loads in their Bergens, which is all well and good if it keeps you comfy, but bad news if it compromises your operational efficiency. Perhaps it's because necessity is the mother of invention, but I think we had it right in the Rhodesian SAS. We marched light, each of us taking a nylon sleeping bag and a pair of trainers in case our boots went down. If I sweated too much, I had a nylon Viet Cong-style suit I could put on at night. Everything was subordinated to three commodities:

water, ammunition and food. Being really ruthless about what we carried gave us maximum time in the bush.

Lots of young soldiers these days put in a lot of time in the gym. All well and good, but physical fitness on its own is not enough. It's time to sweep away the action-movie stuff; fantastic muscle tone and fancy gear is not going to save you in a firefight. You will live or die by your fieldcraft; old-fashioned skills maybe, but it's your ability to close with the enemy and kill him that decides it in the end. In this book I explain a lot of standard operating procedures, tactics and skills that will give you the edge in combat.

But there is more to it than techniques, more to it than excellent levels of fitness. I use the term 'hardness'. A mate of mine is currently serving a thirty-year jail sentence in Zimbabwe. He was part of a team that went in to do a job, but got caught on the Zimbabwe border as they made their getaway they'd been bubbled. The guys had to make a run for it: they got out of the car and cleared off. Three made it, one got caught, an ex-2 Para guy. I asked one of my former colleagues in the Rhodesian SAS what happened, and he said, 'Peter, S— had lost his hardness. He'd been working in a hotel for two years.' It's not something you can put right just by going to the gym. You've got to have that hardness in your soul. Have the bush in your blood, the fresh air in your lungs. There is no substitute for being out there, in the field.

I've divided this manual into four sections. 'Tactics' covers fundamental drills and small-unit drills. 'Theatres of war' examines how different environments and landscapes affect military operations. 'Combat Survival' looks at escape and evasion and general survival skills. 'Marksmanship' explains how to perfect your shooting with rifles, sub-machine guns and pistols. Throughout the manual I will concentrate on small units sections/squads and platoons with a look at company/battalion level where appropriate. This is a manual for front-line soldiering the sharp end so I will not try to explain how to manoeuvre a tank division or run an amphibious invasion. Just bear in mind that the success of every big military operation from D-Day to Desert Storm ultimately depended on the guys in the front-line infantry platoons. However brilliant the plan, whatever weapons and kit have been issued, unless the men are mentally and physically prepared to close with and kill the enemy, the result will be a disaster. In the early 1970s the South Vietnamese Army had overwhelming US airpower to support it and all the latest American kit and was still beaten. In the early 1980s 2 Para attacked the Argentine positions at Goose Green on the Falklands. Against a numerically superior enemy with the same (or better) weapons who had had weeks to prepare the ground, the Paras won the day. Wars are fought with weapons, but they are won by men.

The tactics section concentrates on infantry fighting. Patrolling is probably the single most important skill to get right: it generates intelligence of enemy strengths, dispositions and intentions. Good patrolling can dominate the other side, winning an important psychological advantage, and this applies equally whether you are fighting a professional army or a guerrilla force.

Where you fight obviously has enormous influence on military operations. With few obstacles and practically unlimited fields of fire, the open desert is usually good 'tank country'. Tropical rainforest usually forces everyone to operate on foot; vehicles are restricted to the roads and most air-dropped ordnance is ineffective, even when the aircraft can manage to find the target. However, as we will see, it is not always quite so simple. For instance, the US Army had much more success with its tanks in Vietnam than most people realise. While natural landscapes are important, as this century has progressed more and more fighting has taken place in man-made environments. Many key battles from World War Two to the present day took place in towns and cities. The 'urban battlefield' is becoming increasingly common as cities expand all over the world.

I touch on the subject of survival primarily for soldiers trying to escape and evade. Survival training has improved a great deal in recent years, and has become more than just a 'sickener' designed to test your stamina/enthusiasm. The last section of the manual deals with something that seems increasingly unfashionable in today's anti-hunting, anti-gun, fat-free, unleaded, low-calorie, vegetarian political climate. This is not the place to get involved in the arguments over gun control, but it says something that at the same time the government is paying compensation to law-abiding citizens whose firearms have been confiscated, there's a guy shot dead by other prisoners in the Maze supposedly the country's foremost top-security jail!

INTRODUCTION

From basic battle drills to desert warfare, patrolling techniques to marksmanship, we need to get back to the fundamentals. Sweep away all the bull that obscures the basic truths. This is the game of war. It's about dying. So forget the sexy black uniforms, satellite navigation kit and all the other gadgets. The job of the infantry is to close with the enemy through fire and manoeuvre and kill him. This manual explains how.

Peter McAleese
Birmingham 1998

1 TACTICS

Prepare for battle

The 'section' (or 'squad' to American-trained armies) is the smallest tactical unit on the battlefield, and most of its actions have been refined into drills, carried out in a standardised fashion. Some armies call it 'eldcraft', others call them 'section battle drills'; however they are labelled, these are absolutely fundamental. However many hi-tech gadgets you have, and whatever specialist training you've qualified in, these section battle drills remain the foundation on which everything else follows. The success of all really élite units, from the SAS to the US Navy SEALs, stems from their total mastery of the following drills, not from black uniforms, weird weapons or other exotic kit. The British Army has six basic drills for the infantry section:

1. Preparation for battle
2. Reaction to enemy fire
3. Locating the enemy
4. Winning the firefight
5. Attack
6. Reorganisation

Learning to perform these drills is bloody tedious hard work. And it's what separates effective soldiers from the rest. Each drill is hammered home, practised repeatedly until it becomes a conditioned response, something that is truly second-nature and can be performed with little or no conscious thought. After the shooting starts, there are no action replays. You cannot afford a split-second's hesitation, wondering what to do. By acting instinctively as follows, you should have the edge.

PREPARATION FOR BATTLE

The British Army has a useful mnemonic for preparing for battle: PAWPERSO. It works as follows:

P: Protection
You might be preparing for battle, but what if the enemy is

ready now? While you and your men get sorted out, put a sentry out, ready to warn you if the enemy approaches. Get everyone under cover if possible.

A: Ammunition
Draw and distribute ammunition. Fill and check magazines. One man in each fire team or section can prime the grenades for the whole unit at a safe distance away from everyone else. The section second-in-command should carry a reserve of ammunition if possible. Make sure you can get at your ammunition while lying down; if you hang ammo pouches on the front of your belt, you will have to roll on to your side to get at them, presenting the enemy with a bigger target.

W: Weapons
Check, clean and camouflage your weapons. Set your sights at 300 metres.

P: Personal camouflage
Make sure that your personal camouflage matches the sort of vegetation you are going to be moving through. You'll want enough camouflage to break up your silhouette, but not so much you can't get at your equipment. Check your webbing does not restrict your movement either, and make sure everything is secured so you don't rattle as you move.

Points of Reference
To indicate a target or location to your section, give the information in the order range–direction–reference point e.g. '500-2 left-Church'

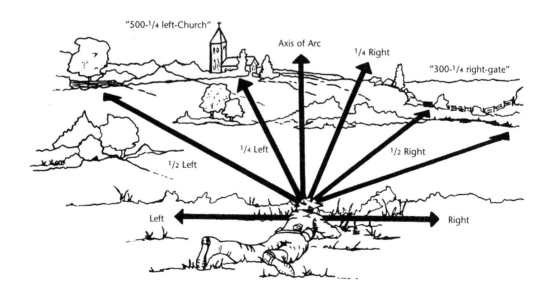

TACTICS

E: Equipment
Check and test any specialist equipment from night-vision devices to first-aid kit. (I'll look at this in more detail later, when we look at patrolling.)

R: Radio
Check all radios are working and that you have spare batteries. Flat batteries or radios on the wrong net have caused more disasters in the last fifty years than almost any other single factor.

S: Service support
Check that you have the correct quantities of rations and water, and that any transport arrangements are still firm.

O: Orders
A section commander's orders are:
1. Reference points
2. Situation: enemy and friendly forces
3. Attachments/detachments
4. Mission
5. Execution
6. Tasks for machine guns and anti-tank weapons
7. Service support
8. Command and signals

The clock ray method
To help identify more difficult targets, use the clock ray method. Give the range then direction as normal, then a number from 1-12 as if there was a clock face around one of the reference points, e.g. '200-4 Left-house-3 o'clock-small tree.'

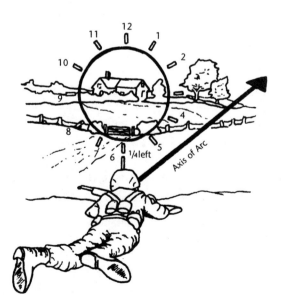

Reference points are vital. Look at the ground over which you are about to move and for each landmark give the range, direction, description and the name by which you will refer to it. For instance, '400 half left path leading towards the woods to be known as "track"'. The purpose of this is for everyone to be using the same terms for the same areas of ground. It's no good someone yelling out that the enemy is coming 'down the track' if there are several tracks visible from your position.

REACTION TO ENEMY FIRE

Before you move off, look at the ground and plan what you will do if you come under fire. The basic principle is to 'keep one foot on the ground', i.e. while half the section moves, the other half stays still, watching over weapon sights, ready to open fire. Make sure everyone is clear what you plan to do, e.g. 'if we come under fire within the next 400 metres, Delta fire team will take cover there and Charlie fire team will fire and manoeuvre forward to the hedgerow'. When you come under fire you have to react instinctively. That is why you practise again and again; it has to be a 'conditioned response', not something you are going to have to think about. There is a mnemonic for this think of 'Dr David Kossoff':

D: Dash
Keep looking out for cover as you move along. So when the enemy opens fire, you don't have to stop and look for cover, you dash like mad to get behind it.

D: Down
Don't dash more than about five metres or you will be shot. Get down.

C: Crawl
Once you are down, crawl along a bit before firing back. If an enemy had you in his sights when you hit the deck, he will be aiming at that spot. Don't stick your head up straight into his next bullet.

O: Observe
Now you must find out exactly where the enemy is. There is no future in simply hiding, nor is there any point shooting indiscriminately. Don't 'spray and pray', you will rarely hit anything.

S: Sights
When you see the enemy, set your sights to the correct range. In the heat of battle this is often forgotten, so it has to be an automatic response and part of your drills.

F: Fire
Fire *aimed* rounds at the enemy. 'Spraying and praying' is not

TACTICS

enough; you have to hit the target. I've seen soldiers shooting steadily and dropping far more guys than the ones that have turned on the hosepipe. I always think of an SAS guy in Borneo: there were Indonesians firing on automatic all over the place brrrrrrrrrrr, brrrrrrrrrrr and Geordie was giving it 'bang ... bang ... bang'. You can guess who won the firefight.

This should be an instant response, but the moment real bullets start coming your way everybody slows down. Just make sure that you don't slow down as much as the other guys.

LOCATING THE ENEMY

This is the hardest battle drill to master, not least because peacetime training rules mean you don't get much live ammunition fired directly at you. Also, a switched-on enemy will wait until you are right out in the open before opening fire. Once you have taken cover, the enemy might well cease fire until you present a better target. However, the 'crack' and 'thump' of the enemy's bullets should give you an idea of which direction he is firing from. Bullets are supersonic, so as they pass over you there is a distinctive 'crack' this is the sound you hear on a rifle range when you are working the butts. After you hear the 'crack', you will hear a 'thump' the noise of the weapon being fired. Sound travels at about 600 metres per second, so if there is a gap of about a second between the 'crack' and the 'thump', the enemy is about 600 metres away. There are three steps to take to locate the enemy:

1. Observe
Study the obvious areas of cover in the direction you think the fire is or was coming from. Look for smoke from weapons (which is why you haven't over-oiled your own) and for disturbed vegetation. The enemy might have had to cut away some of the vegetation to get a clear arc of fire. Poor camouflage discipline might let you see items of equipment or radio antennae.

2. Fire
If the enemy ceases fire and you have not spotted his position within about thirty seconds, put a burst into the most suspect areas. If you get lucky, you will hit the enemy's position (or

come close enough) so that he thinks he's been spotted and returns fire.

3. Movement
If you still cannot locate the enemy, someone will have to stand up and risk getting shot at. The best bet is for the men at either end of the section to double forward about ten metres. They could be nearly 100 metres apart if you are well spread out so the enemy cannot catch them in the same burst. A man dashing for a short distance presents a very hard target because you have barely time to get him in your sights before he has hit the deck again. If this does not trigger any reaction, then the section resumes the advance in short bounds, making very sure to keep one foot on the ground, one team covering while the other moves.

WINNING THE FIREFIGHT

Serving with the Rhodesian SAS, I took part in the airborne assault on Chimoio, a massive ZANLA guerrilla base in Mozambique. The enemy base extended over some twenty-eight kilometres. We had landed in the middle, scattering the guerrillas in panic, and we wanted to find as many as possible before we had to leave. Forty were hiding in a ravine and a brief firefight flared up until their resistance collapsed under the discipline of our fire orders: good, individual fire-and-movement and accurate shooting.

Perhaps you don't have any problem locating the enemy: your advance has triggered a massive firefight. How do you come out on top?

Many firefights are decided in the first few moments. Stunned by the overwhelming volume and accuracy of the enemy's fire, the soldiers on one side start to take cover rather than firing back. It's a vicious circle: the more men take cover, the less firepower the unit puts out, so the enemy's shooting improves. If you can win the firefight, you can close with the enemy and destroy them.

It is not a question of blazing away as fast as you can in the general direction of the enemy. Even when you have suppressed the enemy by accurate shooting, you need good fire control to concentrate your shooting on enemy machine gun positions and/or crew-served weapons. You need to deliver

TACTICS

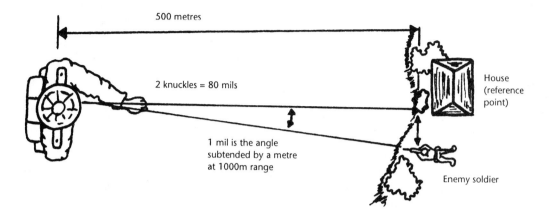

Winning the firefight
The enemy soldier is approximately 500 metres distant. Since 1 mil = 1 metre at 1000m, 80 mils at 500 metres equates to 40 metres. The enemy soldier is 40 metres to the right of the house.

enough firepower to keep the enemy cowering behind cover or at the bottom of a trench while your assault team moves forward to attack. It is a strange fact, proved by a great deal of research, that many soldiers do not fire their weapons unless personally threatened at close range, or they know the sergeant is right next to them. The solution is to train hard, train thoroughly so that the response to a fire order is automatic. This is what made a big difference in the Falklands. The Argentine soldiers, training on firing ranges against bull's-eye targets, found a world of difference between their peacetime practice and the reality of shooting people in front of their position. British soldiers, taught to shoot a man-shaped Figure 11 target whenever it pops up from the bracken, just followed their drills.

Each soldier in a fire team is given an arc to cover, and you have already agreed reference points and their ranges as described above. When you are ordered to fire, set your sights to the correct range, make the weapon ready, and if you cannot see the target yet, shout 'Not seen!' You will probably find yourself watching the section commander's tracer as he indi-

You can use your fingers and knuckles to give approximate numbers of mils for the purposes of estimating horizontal distances between two points. Note that these are averages and if you have unusually small or large hands, you will need to work out what the equivalents are for you.

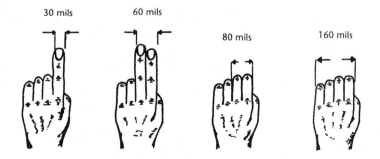

cates the target by firing at it himself. Fire as soon as the command 'Fire!' is given. If the enemy was moving about when the order was given, he will be on the deck in a moment and you must make the most of a good target when you get one. Unless you are very close to the enemy, shoot rapid, aimed semi-automatic shots rather than fully automatic. If the enemy you are firing at does drop to the ground, it is usually difficult to tell whether he has been hit or is just taking cover. So fire again where he went to ground. This may seem ruthless, but this is not a sport.

Good fire control means getting the maximum result from the minimum expenditure of ammunition. With modern weapons, you can fire off vast amounts of ammunition very quickly, but as Rommel, the 'Desert Fox', observed, 'Victory goes to the man with the last round in the magazine.' Fire control orders are given as follows; the mnemonic is GRIT:

G: Group
Which group (re team or part of the section) is going to fire.

R: Range
Pause, and then give the range in metres.

I: Indication
Give the direction of the target by one of the usual methods, e.g. the clock face technique. If all else fails, 'Watch my tracer'.

T: Type of fire
After another pause for everyone to take aim, shout out the type of fire you want. Everyone should be ready to deliver 'deliberate' fire unless otherwise instructed. If the section commander wants 'rapid', it is up to him to order it.

And on the order 'Fire!', the section fires while the section commander observes the effect of the fire. Tension is going to be running high if you are about to issue a fire order for real, not on exercise. So think CLAP your orders must be *clear, loud* and with *pauses* so everyone can follow them.

We choppered in to within twenty kilometres of guerrilla camp 'DK' and walked in at night. It was pissing with rain, which helped us. We finished by crawling forward under cover of the storm. When we stood up, we were right on the edge of the camp and the sweep started. We had about four or five contacts before we realised these guys weren't just terrs, they were conventionally trained soldiers. Lots of our guys couldn't see where the enemy was and for a moment the situation really hung in the balance. I gave a fire order, 'Range: 200 metres; indication: watch my tracer; type of fire: rapid'. All seen! Rapid! And we just wiped them out. There were a lot more of them than there were of us. But we isolated them into pockets and shot it out with each one in turn, bringing the fire of a whole SAS squadron to bear on each position in succession. If they'd have fought in one group, we would have had trouble beating them, but by proper application of basic drills we won. We did the same at Chimoio and Tenby, where instead of fighting as a group the enemy bomb burst out of the position.

THE ATTACK

You are winning the firefight. The enemy's shooting is erratic: it's time to attack. The section commander must give his orders clearly so that everyone knows what they're supposed to be doing. The trick is to keep enough fire on the enemy to enable part of the section to get to close quarters. Whether your section is divided into a 'gun group' and a rifle group, or into two equal fire teams, the principle is the same. One team maintains a base of fire while the other manoeuvres, ideally delivering its final assault at ninety degrees to the line of fire: that means the supporting fire can continue right up to the final moments of the attack.

The rule of thumb used by Western armies is that you need odds of about 3:1 for an attack to work. So a section can take on a single trench with two or three guys in it. In reality, it depends enormously on the training of the troops involved. In Rhodesia we often attacked larger groups of guerrillas, confident that superior training (and air support) would win the day. At the battle of Goose Green, the Paras were outnumbered by the Argentine defenders.

So the support fire keeps most of the enemy hiding in their trench, and only a hardy few have the bottle to shoot back. You have got as close as you can without getting hit by your supporting fire. If you can get near enough to 'post' a grenade into the enemy trench, that is an excellent way to start the bloodthirsty business of close quarter battle. But don't start lobbing grenades about otherwise: you and your team are far more vulnerable out in the open than the enemy in his trench. This really is the moment of truth: to have the sheer courage and professionalism to get in among the enemy with the bayonet. Oh, you will probably do all the damage with a rifle on full auto, but having that bayonet fixed and being confident of killing someone with it makes all the difference. Bayonet attacks are ninety-nine per cent psychological, it is very unusual to actually slug it out man-to-man: someone usually runs before it gets to that point.

REORGANISATION

The moment you have taken the enemy position, start to reorganise. Perversely, it is in this moment of victory that you are at your most vulnerable. Your section is probably scattered, you are likely to have taken casualties, and some guys are low on ammunition. So re-group: allocate arcs of fire to the survivors and re-distribute ammunition if you can't get fresh supplies forward immediately. Allot some guys to deal with the wounded while everyone else watches their arcs and/or improves their positions. You may want to move forward off the exact location of the enemy position: a switched-on enemy will have DF'd his own position and the moment the area is deemed lost, call down an artillery bombardment.

Patrols

'Patrolling is the basis of success. It not only gives the eyes to the side that excels at it and blinds its opponents, but through it the soldier learns to move confidently in the element in which he works.'

Field Marshal Lord Slim, Defeat into Victory

My first contact was during a fighting patrol in Aden with B Squadron SAS. Our mission was to patrol into the Jebel Barash and establish a squadron patrol base from which we were to dominate the area and make our presence felt. On our way in, we bumped into a group of FLOSY (Yemeni guerrillas) who shot our patrol commander. I shot the Arab. Six times. Then all hell let loose with tracer zipping past and grenades going off. A Mills bomb landed with a fierce crack at my feet. Only the detonator had gone off. We were using white phos (phosphorus) to illuminate the wadi and flush the enemy out of cover. At dawn we skirmished through their position, but they had gone, taking their dead and wounded with them. We called in for chopper casevac to extract our two wounded. We then continued our mission and established our intended patrol bases.

Successful patrolling keeps your side up-to-date with information about the enemy and, by the same token, keeps the enemy in the dark about your forces. It enables you to dominate no man's land the ground between opposing front lines and to disrupt and destroy the enemy. In guerrilla war it is often the foundation of victory.

Patrols are tasked with obtaining information or denying it to the enemy. Although patrols will often achieve success by stealth, they must be prepared to fight, either to gain information or just to defend themselves. Patrols are carried out by night and day whether you are attacking or defending. If you are on the defensive, aggressive patrolling will prevent the enemy from learning about your positions. In the Falklands War, the Argentine forces failed to patrol successfully; British patrols were able to get right up to their positions, finding gaps in the enemy minefields and working out the best routes by which to attack.

There are three types of patrol:

Fighting patrols

Fighting patrols are intended to attack the enemy, raiding a key position like a command post, capturing prisoners for intelligence purposes or ambushing enemy units. While many patrols might be undertaken by a four-man team or an eight-man section, fighting patrols are often much larger. The SAS ghting patrol from D Squadron that took out the Argentine airstrip at Pebble Island consisted of over forty men.

Standing patrols

This type of patrol is established to give early warning of enemy movement and to stop enemy patrols infiltrating your defences. Covering ground over which the enemy is expected to approach, they defend their position and call down artillery or mortar fire if the enemy attacks. Typical missions include covering gaps in the enemy minefields (through which the enemy attack would probably come) or keeping dead ground near your position under observation.

Reconnaissance patrols

Reconnaissance patrols rely on stealth, aiming to avoid detection. Ideally, the enemy will have no idea that his positions are discovered. A recce patrol must be prepared to fight, in case it is compromised or gets an unexpected opportunity. Its main objectives are to locate enemy positions and the approaches to them, obtaining as much detail as possible about their layout and the number of men in them. Recce patrols also monitor enemy patrol activity, to find out what areas the enemy thinks is important and where he is concentrating his reconnaissance effort.

PLANNING YOUR PATROL

Proper planning and thorough rehearsal are essential. Everyone must know what action will be taken if you meet the enemy, what formation you will move in, how you will cross obstacles and action on the objective. If you get hit, the rest of the guys must know what is supposed to happen next. When I was doing a patrol I lined everybody up and took them through the whole thing, step by step. I'd say, 'John, what's the first thing we're going to do the minute we leave this position?'

'We're going to move out on a bearing of x amount of mils.'

'Bill, is that correct?'

'Yes.'

'What's next?'

And so on. I'd keep stopping to ask someone else, 'Is that correct?' Why is it not correct?', and keep jumping back and forth. I'd walk along and make it look as if I was working my way along the patrol, then I'd jump back to the first guy. Don't point at someone when you ask a question; ask it to the whole patrol, then ask an individual. That way everyone is trying to think of the answer.

As patrol leader, your aim is to give every guy in your patrol the best deal you possibly can, to prepare and rehearse so thoroughly that the whole thing goes like clockwork. Think and talk through every stage of the patrol and keep asking, 'What if?' Examine every alternative you can imagine so you don't end up trying to improvise a solution to an unforeseen snag in the middle of the night under fire. You must also make arrangements for the reception of the patrol when it returns. Whatever time of day or night you get back, you want shelter from the weather, dry clothes, hot drinks and food. If this is all laid on properly, your debriefing will be more effective and everyone's confidence boosted. Returning exhausted and having to shift for yourself is dispiriting, leading to loss of enthusiasm and reduced efficiency.

In Rhodesia the administration for the men was fairly bad. If a man comes in from patrol and, for morale reasons, there's a hot meal waiting for him, it makes him realise that the people here have actually been thinking about him, had his welfare at heart. I think the guy who really looked after his patrols in the bush was Ron Reid Daly, the commander of the Selous Scouts. When his patrols went into the bush, the Ops officer slept next to the radio he wasn't allowed to leave the radio room in case a patrol got into the shit. That's what you call professionalism. He was outstanding.

You might not have much choice, but when you are selecting your patrol you should weed out anyone with a cold or cough or whose physical fitness or personal reliability could be a problem. You are going to be with a very small team, probably in very close contact with the enemy; to have someone cough his guts up at the wrong moment could endanger the whole patrol.

How you are armed and equipped for a patrol depends on the patrol's task, but beware the temptation to carry less than normal fighting order. You might have to stay out longer than you plan for, so assume you might have to lie up until the next night even if you expect to be back before then.

Choosing your weapons is important too. Fighting patrols have to be able to generate a lot of firepower very quickly, so automatic weapons are essential. The widespread introduction of light machine guns in 5.56mm or 5.45mm calibre makes it no longer necessary to lug about an FN MAG or M60 type 7.62mm GPMG; you can carry so much more ammunition for the smaller calibre weapons that your ability to sustain a firefight is far greater. However, if you are operating in very open terrain the longer range of the 7.62mm machine guns could be important, and extra bulk and weight might be justified. Personal equipment must be double-checked during rehearsals and again before you depart. Everything must be secured so that it does not rattle. While your choice is usually limited by circumstances and what you have been issued with, the following items of special equipment are useful for patrolling:

- telescopic sights/individual weapon sights, or similar
- compass with luminous dial
- watch with concealable luminous face
- binoculars
- shaded torch
- medical kit
- light nylon rope plus toggle ropes
- wire cutters
- masking tape
- thick writing paper and a soft black pencil or white plastic tablet and chinagraph pencil
- image intensifier or any other night-fighting kit available

If you have to reconnoitre a specific area, select one route out and another to return by. Break the journey down into 'legs' of about 1000 metres, and note the magnetic bearing and exact distance. Since you won't be able to measure accurately while actually on the patrol, convert all distances to paces. On patrol, when you are following the compass bearing, get the man behind you to count the paces and someone else to double-check his counting. Try to plan each 'leg' so that it ends with a recognisable terrain feature in sight, something you will be able to identify at night. However, avoid really obvious landmarks which might attract enemy standing patrols, booby-traps or artillery DFs (Defensive Fires). A switched-on enemy will know how tempting it is to use the corner of a wood or track junction to navigate by. He lies in wait, the patrol halts in front of him while the commander checks the bearing of the next leg, and before the commander has looked up from his route card the patrol is shot to pieces. Steer clear of tracks or defiles for the same reason. Nominate an RV (Rendezvous) at the end of each 'leg' so that anyone who becomes separated can rejoin the patrol there.

Make up a route card by writing the distance and bearing of each leg on a piece of transparent plastic using a chinagraph pencil. Tie it around your neck. You can check the route with a beta light underneath (a very dull light source) during short halts. Of course, if the enemy captures it he could follow it straight back to your position, so if you are really devious add or subtract an easily memorable number of metres to all distances on the card, so it will be useless to them. Another trick is to just add a fixed number to all your grid references, but make trebly sure everyone knows what the number is! One other navigational tip is to make sure your compass has been in the daylight as much as possible before a night patrol. That way its luminous dial will glow as brightly as it can.

This is going to sound obvious, but I have to mention it nevertheless. I've known patrol commanders to intentionally give the wrong grid reference over the radio. They get behind schedule, but they don't want to admit this to their seniors. Hoping to make up time on the next leg, they call in the location they are supposed to have reached rather than where they actually are. Whatever pressure you are under to get results, don't give a false grid reference. You are just asking for trouble, and if you do end up in the crap, any support you might have received will be heading in the wrong direction.

In addition to using false distances on your route card so it would be useless to an enemy, you should make sure the opposition does not capture your compass with its current setting still on. I was once on an SAS escape and evasion exercise in Wales. We were supposed to have broken out from a prisoner-of-war camp and were heading for the coast. But the security forces picked us up one by one, and their intelligence guys compared the settings on each recapt-ured man's compass. Plotting the thing on the map revealed that the escapees were all making for the same point. Moral of the tale: if you are about to be captured, twist the compass to a new setting.

If it is humanly possible, rehearse the whole patrol over ground as similar to that where you will be operating. This is the time to find out that the night-sights don't work or that no one has any wire cutters, not in the middle of the night close to an enemy position. Ideally, a night patrol should be rehearsed by night as well as by day. All the following actions should be rehearsed.

- order of march and individual positions in all formations to be used
- how you intend to cross obstacles
- action on entering a minefield
- action if someone triggers a booby-trap or trip-flare
- action on meeting the enemy, both on the way out and the way back
- action on the objective
- action at halts and RVs including Final RV
- signals to be used
- plans to deal with casualties
- plans to deal with prisoners
- how you will return to your own position without attracting 'friendly fire'

Of course this is rather a counsel of perfection. You may not have time to properly rehearse everything, but you must at least rehearse your actions on the objective. When you give the patrol your orders, let every member of the patrol ask questions. Pose them a few questions too. Everyone must know exactly what he is going to do, including who will take over from whom if you suffer casualties.

Before setting out, carry out a detailed final inspection:

1. Check that weapons have been test-fired and zeroed, and that you have the right ammunition in the right quantities.

2. Ensure you have both WP and HE grenades.

TACTICS

3. Ensure your equipment doesn't rattle and your clothing doesn't rustle.

4. Make sure no one is carrying any papers, letters or other material that would provide intelligence to the enemy.

5. Check that faces and hands are properly camouflaged.

6. Check that the radio has fresh batteries, is on net and does work.

7. Make sure you are carrying first field dressings and morphine and in the same pocket by every man, so you can find someone's shell dressing when they're incapacitated.

8. Check that any items of special kit are working.

Make sure you test every bit of kit you are bringing along, even if it's really simple. For instance, if you're going to mark something or tie something up with some string, check that whoever's carrying it can pull the string out without tangling it up. Maybe you'll have to make up a bobbin for it. On one patrol in Africa we were going to have to cut our way through a wire fence, but in rehearsals someone asked how often the fence was patrolled by the enemy. We thought every half-hour, so we took some extra wire with us to hide the gap we cut. You find this sort of thing out on rehearsals.

I get the guys to line up and go through all the kit. 'OK, what are you carrying?'

He'll stand there and say, 'A claymore, 200 rounds of ammunition and so on and so on.'

'Are you carrying any tracer?'

'No.'

'Why not?'

Then I'll say to someone, 'Check my kit.' I'm not having a go at anyone, it's just that in my experience this sort of dialogue is the best way to make sure (a) you don't forget anything, and (b) guys will come up with some useful ideas. Getting ten people working on the subject is bound to generate more solutions. There are few things worse than going out on a job and finding that you need something you haven't got. I've learned this the hard way.

In *Bravo Two Zero*, Andy McNab keeps on about 'check and test, check and test', but on that ill-fated patrol they obviously didn't do so thoroughly. It doesn't matter what unit you're in, you can't get this over just by the way you stand. How come they were carrying 200 pounds of kit and no one thought to pack a jumper? How come the radios packed up? How was it that they never looked back and so the patrol became fragmented? They'd clearly not prepared for it. I've spoken to people who were on that briefing, and apparently when one guy asked about the ground, he was told 'Well, it's desert.' I'm sorry, but that's just not good enough, especially when you think that that was a composite patrol, guys that were not used to working with each other. Why did the sergeant-major not sit in on that briefing? I'd have asked them if there was anything they needed, and asked to have a look at their immediate action drills. Also, why did people feel they couldn't question what was going on? I'm not being critical for the sake of it, but that patrol led to needless loss of lives. In this book I might seem a bit harsh on special forces, but that's where I've spent most of my career. Remember that, today, the British Army seems to be slavishly following everything the SAS does, but who's to say the SAS have got it all right? I am just concerned that we're losing the ability to question what we're doing. Blind self-confidence is a very dangerous thing. And only the self-important can't take criticism.

You have to see or hear the enemy before he hears or sees you. This can be a severe test of patience as well as physical fitness, since you must move silently and stay switched on at all times. You have to maintain a high standard of observation and frequent halts are vital. Stop, look and listen for two or three minutes. Everyone observes his arc with maximum vigilance. Remember that at night, your ears can be more important than your eyes. By kneeling or lying down you can often see more, as men and vehicles are silhouetted against the skyline. Image intensifiers and other night-sights are extremely useful, but the enemy might well have better ones, so do not rely too heavily on the hardware, or think it gives you an advantage.

Keep your concentration. It's the details that matter, especially when you're cold and wet and tired. You know the situation: the guys are knackered, you see a nice gap in the fence or wall, and you think 'fuck it', and go through rather than do it the hard way. I have a friend who lost both legs because he ignored his obstacle-crossing drills. His patrol came to a fence and drove through the gap, which turned out to be mined and the vehicle blew up. You get the same thing in Northern

TACTICS

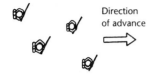

File
This is the best formation to adopt when following linear features, especially at night. The patrol commander and scout are the first pair, the 2-i-c and gunner form the second pair in a four man patrol.

Single File
The easiest formation to control, but you have little firepower available ahead or behind.

Arrowhead
A useful formation for a full section moving over open ground: you can bring down fire to both flanks or straight ahead with the minimum of fiddling about..

Ireland all the time: you come to a thick hedgerow, all of a sudden there's a gap in the hedge and you can see the fence across it. There's a step. And that's where you'll find the booby-trap. Get your obstacle-crossing drills sorted out and stick to them no matter if you're tired or running behind schedule or whatever.

When selecting a position in which to halt, make sure to avoid obvious topographical features these might be RV points for an enemy patrol. A halt gives the patrol commander a valuable opportunity to check the map. Sometimes the patrol will have to halt for longer. You might want to stop for fifteen minutes or so to answer calls of nature, establish comms or just take a short break. If you are going to halt for longer than a few minutes, you need to do more than just observe your arcs. Don't just halt where you are; if someone is following you he could follow your track to arrive on top of you. Instead, loop around your track and establish an immediate ambush. Deploy for all-round defence. You can remove your Bergen, but no more. Keep your belt kit on and your weapons ready. However long you halt for, it is vital to have a clearly agreed signal for moving off and to check that everyone knows it. Otherwise you will leave people behind.

If your route takes you along the edge of a wood, move inside it, parallel to the edge rather than staying in the open. It will be harder to move quietly, but considerably safer. Avoid skylines wherever possible. Streams, tracks, fences or other obstacles present special problems. Sod's Law says that you will have a contact when you are divided by a thick hedge or similar. When you reach an obstacle, halt, lie down and listen. If there is no sign of the enemy, carry on as planned, applying the rules of fire and manoeuvre: no one moves unless he is covered by another member of the patrol. Halt again when the patrol has crossed the obstacle, look and listen to see if you have been detected.

Patrols can use three basic formations, and each has its pluses and minuses. If you move in single file it is much easier to stay in contact in woods or dense vegetation, but it is easy to switch off and just follow the bloke in front, leading to nasty surprises if the enemy is on the other side. A single line takes time to put down fire ahead or behind and it takes ages to pass messages up and down. As a rule it is best to avoid single lines if there are more than four of you, unless you are moving along a hedgerow or similar feature, or operating in

Diamond
Excellent night formation when crossing open ground, this gives you all-round firepower.

The 'blob'
Not so much a formation as a mass of men crammed up close. Highly vulnerable if the enemy opens fire, but useful for rushing across a track in the dark. At night it can also look like a bush or shadow when you all lie down.

the jungle. Moving in file is the second option; this gives better all-round protection than single file. The third is diamond formation: difficult to control in close cover, it provides the best all-round observation/firepower on open ground.

Supposing you do find the enemy, say a group of armoured cars camouflaged at the edge of a wood. Once you have studied the position and slipped back to your rendezvous, have a brief discussion with the rest of the patrol. Someone may have spotted something you missed. You need to pass the information back up the chain of command immediately. To do this quietly and without shining torches all over the place, crawl into your sleeping bag while the rest of the patrol adopts all-round defence. Using a pencil torch (mini-Maglite, or better, something like a Petzl zoom torch that you can fit to a headband, leaving both hands free) mark everything you have seen on your map. Then send back your radio report. Don't rush it in your excitement and encode the signal incorrectly. This is the time to decide if your planned withdrawal route should be revised in the light of what you have discovered. Make your decision, switch off the torch and get back out of the sleeping bag. Wait for your night vision to return before setting off again.

When you return to your own front line, circle around to make sure you have not been followed. One of the oldest tricks in the world is to infiltrate an enemy position by tagging on to the back of returning patrols: the enemy will either attack straight away or might just sit close enough to hear the sentry's challenge and the patrol's reply. Having checked you are alone, approach the friendly position, identify yourself and advance to be recognised.

Navigation checklist

1. Keep each leg of the patrol no more than 1500 metres long.

2. Note the magnetic bearing of every leg, even the shortest.

3. Note a right and left boundary for each leg so you can tell if you have wandered off track.

4. Pick RVs you can find in darkness; for instance, pick a wall 100 metres in front of the second RV and a stream behind it. If you reach the stream, you know you have overshot.

5. Appoint a 'check navigator' to read the map and provide an

independent check on your navigation. I prefer to use two guys with cattle counters, clicking every 100 paces, and another guy behind me checking the navigation. The counters also serve as flankers since when you're concentrating on moving along a bearing, you aren't very well aware of your surroundings. That is a good thing about diamond formation: your firepower is lined up either side of you.

6. Note the terrain features you should be able to see on each leg.

7. If there are no features to observe, it is difficult to maintain an exact bearing, so get the second-in-command to check his compass too from the back of the patrol.

PATROL S.O.P.S. (STANDARD OPERATING PROCEDURES)

There is rarely enough time to rehearse a military operation as thoroughly as you would like. So infantry training includes SOPs for all manner of situations. Practised regularly, they enable well-trained infantry to tackle most problems with a minimum of special preparation. As the saying goes, 'train hard, fight easy'. Make sure the following 'actions on' become second nature and can be accomplished immediately, without further orders:

1. Finding a trip-wire
Don't hang about to find out whether it's connected to a claymore or a flare. Withdraw carefully, making sure to find any others before they find you. Get back to your last RV and re-think your route.

2. Hitting a trip-flare
If you set off a trip-flare you have no more than a second or two before the enemy deluges the area with machine gun fire and detonates his claymores. If you're paying attention, you'll hear the thing going up before it detonates. Bomb-burst out of the killing ground then run back to your last RV. It is for exactly this situation that you have RVs built into your patrol route.

3. Finding yourself in a minefield
A well-trained enemy will cover a minefield with fire, so when one of your patrol steps on a mine and is killed or wounded, the enemy will then rake the area with small-arms fire. If you are under fire, you have no choice but to fire and manoeuvre

back, taking the casualty with you and hoping no one steps on another one. You cannot remain where you are or you will all die anyway. If the minefield is not covered by fire, prod your way out carefully the same way you came in. Mark the position of the minefield on your map.

4. Caught in the light
If you are in the open when the enemy lets off a parachute flare or fires an illumination round, drop to the ground immediately. If you are moving through vegetation, say tall grass or open woodland, slowly crouch down; under the wobbling light of a parachute flare it is very hard to spot slow movement, but a fast move such as someone diving for the deck is seen more easily.

5. Someone is hit
Another one you have to work out on rehearsal and not 'on the night'. If you are in a four-man patrol and one of the guys goes down, it will take two of you to pull him out, so your firepower is down to one man. While you will plan to extract your wounded, there may be exceptions such as someone getting injured right at the start of the patrol, e.g. breaking an ankle in a rabbit hole. In that situation, you could leave them to be picked up on the way back, or by a standby patrol from your own front line. On the other hand, your rehearsals might show that you need every man to do the job, and an early casualty would force you to abort.

6. Taking a prisoner
Detail a couple of the biggest, strongest men to guard any prisoners you take. Ideally, you should bring plasticuffs and some sort of hoods with which to blindfold the POWs.

7. You get separated from the rest of the patrol
Go back to the place you last saw each other. Wait for about half an hour. If no one returns by then, head back on your own.

8. The whole patrol becomes lost
Memorise the major landmarks and local road/track network so you have a rough idea of the way back even if you wander out of your patrol area.

Have confidence in your navigation. In the SAS in Borneo I was on a training operation and the old jungle soldiers kept pumping in to me, 'If you get lost, go back to where you last knew where you were.' We were set to go along this ridge, but I said, 'We've already done this,' and added that we ought to go back to where we last knew for certain where we were. There was a little dispute in the patrol and this guy says, 'I'm not going with you.' (I was the patrol CO.) I said, 'It's your choice.' I went back to where I last knew where I was, worked it out and found our way back to camp. This guy didn't wander in until the next day.

9. Contact with the enemy

Whether you see the enemy before he sees you will obviously depend on the size of your patrol and its orders. The important thing is that you know what you will do in specific situations. The patrol commander simply has to give a short order, usually nothing more than the signal for a hasty ambush, or to sit tight. If you are doing a recce, you will probably want to allow the enemy past and observe. A ghting patrol will probably mount an ambush. If you are not sure if they have seen you, assume they have. If you and the enemy spot each other at the same time, whoever has thought his answer out in advance will have the drop on the other guy. If the enemy sees you first, you don't want to have to stop and think.

It is worth stating at this point that it is just as dangerous to do more than you are tasked with than less. Just get the job done and come back; do not start adding to the mission because you spot some target of opportunity. I knew a good soldier in Africa who was notorious for swanning off on his own bat in the middle of a patrol. He'd think, 'That looks interesting', but he wouldn't remember to inform headquarters, he'd just take his patrol maybe ten or fifteen kilometres off their assigned area because he wanted to check something out. It really pissed off the guys with him, who had completed their task, and risked anything from a 'blue-on-blue' to an encounter with the enemy in which his patrol would have had no support.

PATROL HARBOURS

If you are going to stop for more than half an hour, you should follow the procedure for setting up a patrol harbour. This procedure is mainly used for lying-up by day or night, with the patrol in an all-round defensive position. The first thing to do is to get off the track. However carefully you have been mov-

Patrol Harbour
The Platoon assumes an all-round defensive position while a recce team goes forward to check the proposed site of the patrol harbour. The platoon commander, scouts, section commanders and radio operator go forward, leaving a sentry to mark the entry point into the wood. The platoon commander shows the section commanders where they will deploy their men.

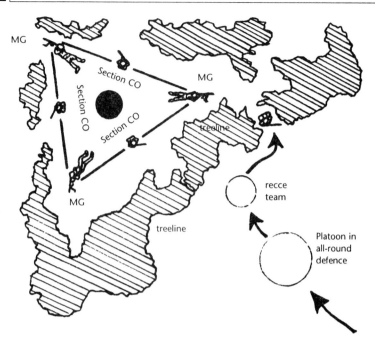

ing, you are bound to have left some sort of trail that an observant enemy might be able to follow by daylight. You need to vanish. So instead of moving directly into the site selected for your patrol harbour, come parallel to it and all turn together. Then, moving with the utmost care, twisting and turning to avoid snagging vegetation, move off your track. If anyone has been clever enough to follow your tracks, he will now advance past your position rather than right into it.

Don't move straight into your patrol harbour. I prefer to use two sites: one in which you carry out your administration, cooking etc., and one in which you will actually get your head down. Once your admin is completed, and it is totally dark, move into your patrol harbour. Again, wait ten minutes or so, listening carefully. If the enemy is on to you, he will make noise as he crashes about in the undergrowth. If all's well, get your heads down. Use light sticks to guide a large patrol into the harbour. I once put 116 guys into a defensive position at night using light sticks to guide everyone. We only had green light sticks in Africa, but we saved coloured sweet wrappers and used the different coloured cellophane to give a variety of colours. Nowadays you can get mini-light sticks in all sorts of colours.

When selecting a site for your patrol harbour, the most important consideration is cover and concealment. If

TACTICS

The Platoon enters the wood in single file. To occupy the patrol harbour, each man is put into position at the start of his section's side of the triangle. Machine guns are placed at the corners for maximum arcs of fire. The Platoon HQ is located in the middle of the triangle.

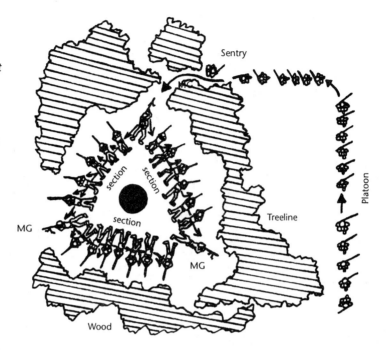

attacked, your aim is to break contact and get away, not to fight a defensive action. After your move into your chosen position, stop for fifteen minutes and listen for the enemy. If there are no suspicious sounds, remove your Bergens and put them in front of you, everyone continuing to cover his arc. Depending on the ground and the size of your patrol, you might want to send out part of your force to patrol the immediate area around the patrol harbour, just in case the enemy is closer than you think. On the other hand, such 'clearing patrols' can often attract attention they make more noise and leave more evidence of your presence.

Many manuals will tell you rations should be eaten cold as cooking smells can travel a very long way. But if you've tried living on cold rations for days on end, you'll know that this is really bad news. South Africa's 32 Battalion did six-week trips and you can't eat cold rations for that long. In my experience you can get away with cooking. In Rhodesia, we scraped a hole in the ground to keep the flame from the hexy block out of sight. This is another reason why we preferred to do our admin/cooking in one area near dusk, then move into the patrol harbour proper once it was completely dark. Anyone sneaking up on where we'd been cooking would miss us, but we'd hear them.

If you are stopping to sleep, kip in a bivi bag but do not build

Clearing Patrols

After the position is occupied, you need to double-check no-one is following you, so stop and listen for 10 minutes or so. Then send out clearing patrols to make sure no enemy are in the immediate area. Work around the triangle in three sectors, at the limit of visibility. Each clearing patrol moves out through one corner gun position and returns to the next. Make sure each patrol travels counter-clockwise so they don't blunder into each other or approach a gun position from an unexpected direction. You want to be certain that there are no enemy close enough to hear or see you: a minimum distance of 300 metres.

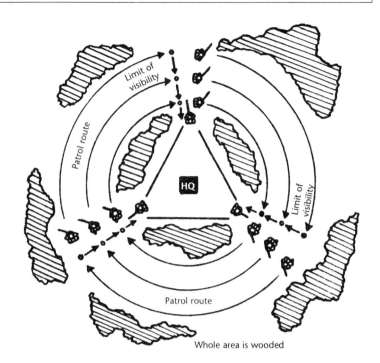

Whole area is wooded

bashas. Do not remove your boots; if the enemy does bump your position, he won't give you time to put them back on. Keep stag in rotation, each man waking up his neighbour and so on round the position. This saves movement, no one having to blunder about in the dark to alert the next guy for sentry duty. If you doubt the reliability of your soldiers to take turns on stag, allocate the duty in pairs and make sure the change-overs overlap.

In the morning, stand-to, pack your kit and move off as soon as it is light. Go into another admin harbour after an hour or so. That's where you have breakfast, not on the site of your overnight position. Your aim in the morning is to get away from there as soon as you can, just in case you have been picked up.

While long-range patrols using only four or five men are possible, and widely practised by the SAS, they are only feasible for the most highly trained and motivated soldiers. If the objective is, say, thirty kilometres from the front line, it is more usual to send a thirty-man platoon to conduct the patrol. Although the actual patrolling of the objective might be accomplished by a four-man team, the rest of the platoon occupies a patrol harbour nearby to support it. That way the patrol can lie up, with security provided by the rest of the platoon. It can undertake its recce of the target area fresh and rested. If it gets into trouble, it can fall back on the platoon which is far more able to fight its way out of difficulty than four men on their own.

A platoon patrol harbour follows the same principles. The commanding officer must recce the position himself, then brief the section commanders. If you are doing this, send on a small party ahead to provide additional security. You have just concentrated all the leadership in one place, and if the enemy attacked at that moment command and control would be impossible. The best layout, used by the Australian SAS in Vietnam, is in the form of a triangle with light machine guns at the corners and the platoon headquarters in the middle. The sections should be about twenty metres from the centre. Get everyone into position and then have a listening halt for fifteen minutes or so. Then send out three-man clearing patrols to check around the perimeter. If a whole platoon is going to be in place for any length of time, you have to examine your surroundings carefully. Note that this is where the value of repeated rehearsals comes in; with unpractised troops the clearing patrols might well fire on each other or get shot at when they return to the harbour.

While you do not want to disturb the ground too much, it is worth clearing your fields of fire so that everyone can shoot without the aim being obscured by vegetation. Post sentries just within hearing of the platoon position, so the enemy cannot get close enough to hear you without (hopefully) being spotted by a sentry. Lay comms cord from the sentry positions back to the machine gun posts. You cannot avoid moving about in the position with twenty to thirty men on the site, so clear a track plan and make sure anyone who has to move uses the track. Clear any crunchy vegetation from the floor and snap off twigs or branches at up to head height to create a path that you can use in silence. Lay cord along it, so in pitch darkness you can stick to the path.

If the threat justifies it, everyone should dig a small shell-scrape, excavating just enough earth to get their chest cavity below ground. Resist the temptation to pile up earth in front of you as this will usually appear obvious and will attract fire. The idea is to mould yourself into the natural lie of the land, keeping as low a profile as possible while still being about to cover your arcs. Such a shell-scrape can be concealed in the morning. Anything more ambitious is going to be hard to hide. To shelter from the elements, you can put up a basha. Use a poncho with bungees attached to secure it to the vegetation *but do not put this up until after last light.* Any such shelter creates straight lines, a distinctive silhouette that will stand out like a sore thumb in daylight. If you have them, deploy claymore mines at the corners of the position, with interlocking blast areas to leave no area uncovered. Stand-to just before last light. Once it is fully dark, go over to the sentry routine. There should be no movement on the position other than sentry change-over.

When you leave the site, take all your rubbish with you. Crush tins etc. and pack them in your Bergen. On the most sneaky-beaky patrols you will take your own crap with you in plastic bags, leaving no trace of your presence (except in the jungle, where you can usually get away with crapping).

Patrol base checklist

1. Site the base away from tracks, gullies, streams or habitation.

2. Avoid steep slopes or wet ground where you won't be able to sleep properly.

3. Set up the base just before last light.

4. Concealment is vital, but the base must be in a reasonable defensive position.

5. Rehearse how you will break contact and escape back to a prearranged RV if the enemy attacks the base.

6. Always have your weapon within reach and never go three paces from your webbing.

7. When you have finished with a piece of kit, pack it away. Leave nothing lying about.

8. Don't cook curry or anything else with a strong spicy smell.

9. If you cook on a fire in daylight, it must be smokeless.

10. Sentries should have not one, but two agreed ways of alerting the rest of the base, just in case one does not work, e.g. have comms cord and a field telephone. In fact it's a bad idea to be so far apart you can't just tap each other on the shoulder at night that's how you take over stag anyway.

11. Mark your arcs of fire with sticks or suchlike so they are

obvious even at night.

12. If you suspect your position has been compromised, move. If the enemy locates you, there will probably be some delay while he plans his attack. If you are more alert than him, you should be able to slip away before he realises exactly what he has discovered.

13. Do not clean more than one machine gun at once, so most of your firepower is available at any given time.

OBSERVATION POSTS

An Observation Post (OP) is a position from which you can observe a particular area while concealed from view and enemy fire. OP work is often colder, wetter and more boring than any other military activity, and for that reason it is a real test of soldiering skill. It is very easy to switch off, to allow your attention to wander for a few minutes when you are supposed to be observing, say, a field in South Armagh. And it's always at that moment that the terrorist sniper will move into position. In Rhodesia the security forces achieved some great successes thanks to the enormous professionalism of the Selous Scouts. While spectacular 'externals' against guerrilla bases captured the headlines, it was the unglamorous, covert OP work that built up the intelligence picture on which so many victories depended.

An OP typically consists of a four-man team, and it is vital that you are used to working together. It is intimate, claustrophobic and very wearing, so you have to get along and trust each other.

The first task is to select the site of the OP. Ideally, you want to recce the area in daylight, but in many situations you might have to choose the position from the map, possibly with the aid of aerial photographs. Your priorities are a good view of the ground you are ordered to observe, but with an entry/exit concealed from the enemy. You will hopefully be able to find space behind the OP for an admin base. Avoid isolated cover, like the only clump of trees for miles around, and consider the air threat: if the enemy has air support can your position be detected by helicopter or low-flying aeroplane? Once again, avoid corners of woods or similar landmarks; you don't want your position being used for an enemy patrol's rendezvous. If you can check the lie of the land in daylight, remember to determine what you can see lying down rather than standing up. Do not linger in the area; if the enemy (or civilians with enemy sympathies) see you exploring the area, testing your radio comms etc., then your OP will be compromised before you've even set it up. The best way is to stop on the site during what seems to be a routine patrol.

A good way to set up your OP is to have a large patrol, say platoon strength, move through the area at night. Your four-man team is dropped off, remembering to collect any heavy kit that other patrol members are carrying for you. The rest of the patrol carries on. It is very difficult for the enemy to detect that the patrol is four men short. A similar principle was used in Vietnam to insert OPs by helicopter. A helicopter would hover, as if dropping off a patrol, then take off again, the soldiers lying flat on the helicopter floor so any Viet Cong seeing it would not realise the men were still on board. More 'dummy runs' would follow after the patrol had been dropped off. In Aden we had so many Arab spies around the camp that we dropped off OPs by hiding men in the back of the rubbish wagon. In South Africa we used to leave OPs behind when withdrawing from an assault on a guerrilla camp. The guerrillas would re-occupy the position, and the OP could call in follow-up air strikes.

Once you are on your own on the OP site, go into all-round defence and wait. Listen carefully for any suspicious sounds. If nothing happens for fifteen minutes or so, then start work on the OP. Although it's dark, remember that movement can still be seen, so a useful tip is to erect a screen of black hessian or similar lightweight material around where you are going to dig in. Three men dig while one acts as sentry. Rotate jobs at intervals. Keep the noise down by putting a sandbag over your pick-axe, and if you are using pickets to support the roof of a dug-in OP, pile empty sandbags on top of them before you drive them into the ground. Pile the earth you excavate onto a poncho, for instance, then roll it up and conceal it. You don't want to leave a great pile of earth next to your nicely camouflaged position!

The amount of digging in should be tailored to the level of threat. This is the extreme, favoured by the British Army throughout the Cold War when our OPs were expected to survive on the inner German border in the face of all that Soviet heavy artillery. But digging in leaves a massive trench scar when you withdraw, so you have to resolve the conflict between cover and security. You purchase your safety from heavy artillery at the expense of long-term security. The

British Army view of OPs is still conditioned by Northern Ireland and Germany, but if you are a special forces or recce platoon man, you probably don't want to leave signs that you've been in an OP, so don't dig in. What bigger mess could you leave behind than a damn great trench?

Properly prepared, a good OP position should be invisible to an enemy even when he is practically standing on top of it. The SAS have managed to maintain OPs literally in the enemy's back garden before now. In conventional war, your OP might have to be proof against enemy shell-fire and this means at least 500mm of earth overhead to keep out shell fragments. Make sure your roof follows the natural lie of the land.

You also need to excavate a little trench, up to a metre deep, behind the OP. This is your entrance/exit, concealed from enemy view. It goes without saying that the position needs to be camouflaged thoroughly and that any vegetation you snap off to conceal the OP must be renewed before it dies off. You don't want to be hiding under the one patch of dead bracken in a lush green landscape. Check your camouflage thoroughly just before dawn, then, like Count Dracula, disappear into the dank earth before the first rays of sun strike you.

The standard shape of a dug-in OP is in the form of a cross, with each of you facing outwards. In the middle, where your boots touch, the ground is dug deeper to act as a drain and as a piss tube. As I said, OP work in a European climate is a cold, wet and unpleasant business at most times of the year, but there are steps you can take to keep a little warmer and drier. Wear thermal underwear and down salopettes and a fibrepile jacket which dries out quickly under a breathable Gore-tex type jacket with your combat jacket on top of that. Gore-tex does tend to rustle, so you don't want that as your top layer. One-piece dry suits as used by cave divers can work well too, and chemical hand-warmers are useful, if bulky, items when you need to keep your fingers flexible.

OP kit checklist

For building an OP:
- ponchos
- mini saw
- machetes
- secateurs
- chicken wire

- strong gloves
- cam nets
- face veils
- shovel/pickaxe/entrenching tools
- paracord
- stakes

In the OP:
- personal weapons, immediately accessible
- optical equipment (see below)
- range card
- maps
- pencils
- pocket tape recorder
- medical equipment
- tough plastic gardening-type rubbish bags
- clingfilm or smaller plastic bags
- radio, spare batteries and appropriate code system
- OP log and note sheets to record what you see
- food and water
- spare warm clothing

Optical equipment is essential. Ideally you want several pairs of powerful binoculars, say x10 power, plus a telescope with x60 magnification for close observation of buildings. You will also need a functioning camera with telephoto lens. To keep watch at night, a night scope is extremely useful. The old British Army IWS (Individual Weapon Sight) enables you to pick out a man standing in the open at up to 300 metres, and more modern American kit can do so at twice this distance. However, image intensifiers work by maximising the ambient light and they can be temporarily blinded by flares or search-lights that overload the system. Thermal imagers work by passive infra-red, which means they are not vulnerable to sudden flashes of light, and they can effectively 'see through' camouflage and chemical smoke. A laser range-finder can make life easier too, enabling you to accurately determine the distance to something you observe. (Although some types of tank now have laser warning devices fitted, so checking the range to a Russian T-90 could be dangerously counter-productive!)

When you have to be sure the enemy has no idea you were there, keep a record of all the kit you take with you into the

OP. Log it, and re-check when you leave.

Chris Schullenberg was a captain in the Selous Scouts whose patrol reports were legendary works of art. He lay up near one guerrilla camp, watching all the tracks leading into it, monitoring the traffic. He knew what went in and what went out. Then he looked around for good drop-zone sites in case we wanted to attack it with our airborne units. Where could the helicopters put down? He anticipated what the high command might want to do. He took photos of the approach routes. Then he went right into the camp at night, leaving his weapon with the other guy (I'm talking about a two-man patrol here). He walked in alone, with just a hand grenade. He counted all the bashas, all the huts to give a precise report on the number of enemy present. He took his weapon off, because if anyone fired at him and he fired back, the gooks would know the enemy was there. But if a sentry fired and no one fired back, they'd think they'd fired on one of their own guys by mistake it happens. But if he was really spotted, he'd lob the grenade and know to get down, but the other guy wouldn't. When it went off, he'd have time to leg it into the bush. Schullenberg would watch a camp for ten to fourteen days, identifying every position, the times when sentries changed over, when day routine took over from night routine etc. He discovered that the guerrillas tended to strip and clean all their weapons at the end of a dawn stand-to clearly a good time for us to attack.

OP routine

Swap roles every four hours maximum. If you are looking through binoculars or (worse) image intensifiers, time on stag is sharply reduced. No one can keep his concentration looking through lenses for more than an hour or two. The radio operator keeps a listening watch on the radio and, if you are using observation devices that tire the eyes quickly, he shares observation duty with the observer. The observer scans the target area for about four hours, then wakes up the man on rest and gets some kit or attends to personal admin himself. The man on rest sleeps and deals with personal admin. The sentry keeps an eye on the approaches to the OP so you do not get bumped by the enemy.

Observing does not mean staring into space. Divide the area you are studying into three sections: near, middle ground and far. Look at one, then the next, then the next, sweeping slowly from side to side with the binoculars. Rest your eyes regularly. You can practise your observation skills with the old children's game 'Kim's game'. Look for changes in vegetation: the dried-out plants someone's snapped off to camouflage their position, etc.

Personal admin rarely gets more personal than in an OP. Put simply, there is nowhere to go for a dump. You cannot wander out of the position for a 'shovel recce', you have to go where you are. Hence the clingfilm and plastic bags you brought with you. Wrap the crap well to cut down on smells and flies. Use stacks of insect repellent. Watch what you eat too: this is not the place to get an attack of the runs. If in doubt, eat a packet or two of biscuits AB to bung you up.

We did an ambush in Aden, and if anyone had walked into us that night, it would have been a massacre. We were overlooking a wadi from the bank above, with claymores dug into the bank. It was a full moon and the whole killing ground was naturally illuminated. There we were, sitting in the position, doing all the drills, shitting in bags, keeping all our rubbish tidied away in sandbags to take away with us. Suddenly we heard a noise: there was somebody coming through the rubbish cache behind us. Everybody turns around, safeties off ... it was a baboon! It grabbed the sandbag full of empty ration cans etc. and ran off into the night.

Truly hard men might argue that you cannot cook in an OP as the smell of cooking will betray you. However, it takes a special kind of dedication to live on cold rations alone for several days while lying cramped and cold beneath the ground. A gaz cooker or similar can usually be used to produce the occasional hot drink, if nothing else. This is one of the key reasons why you need to examine potential OP sites carefully. Do you really need to be right on top of the enemy, where cooking could betray you? Could you not do the job from further away, using better telescopic kit? Look at the map. Study the ground. You don't always have to be in the enemy's back yard to see what he is up to.

If your patience is rewarded, and the enemy is spotted, you send off a contact report in the normal manner with a time, map reference, enemy strength (e.g. group of four armoured personnel carriers), enemy direction (e.g. heading south-west along a farm track), your response (e.g. continuing to observe) and any additional information (e.g. vehicle markings/special equipment etc.).

Last point: when you've finished packing up, stuffing all your rubbish into sandbags and leaving not a trace of your presence, have a double-check. It is remarkable how often a final check will reveal a single round of ammunition or whatever, something that could betray the fact that you had an OP in this position.

Ambushes

The word 'ambush' conjures up the idea of soldiers lying stock-still in absolute silence, waiting patiently for the enemy to walk into the trap. Then, without warning, they trigger claymore mines and open up with automatic weapons at point-blank range. This is a *deliberate* ambush, and it can be devastatingly effective, enabling a relatively small force to inflict damage out of all proportion to its size. However, ambushes are not always so carefully planned; sometimes it is possible to organise an *immediate* ambush if the tactical situation allows.

IMMEDIATE AMBUSH

In Angola one member of our patrol had just had his foot blown off on a mine laid beside the road. Then someone at the back of the column shouted the alarm. An enemy vehicle was coming. Our track had just led us across a road and the rear party could see a large Soviet ZIL truck trundling up the road about a mile away. I ran back down the track to the road and rapidly deployed the guys at the back of the column into immediate ambush positions. They ran and hid in the scrub at the side of the dirt road. Someone had dug a trench at the junction of the track and the road.

It's no good ambushing vehicles from the side of the road because the target is too fleeting. When the ZIL truck came up close, I stepped out in full view in the road and blasted the cab head-on with my Galil, smashing the windscreen and raking the three enemy MPLA inside. As it passed, swerving and slowing up, I shot another enemy soldier sitting in the back. The guys in their immediate ambush positions finished the truck off, pumping a fearsome weight of fire into it as it rolled past to a stop.

An immediate ambush is, by definition, something you cannot plan. But you can prepare. Just as we have seen with patrolling techniques, a continued programme of training and detailed rehearsals can build teamwork to the point that detailed orders are not necessary for, say, an immediate linear ambush like our attack on the MPLA.

TACTICS

DELIBERATE AMBUSH

A deliberate ambush is a planned, rehearsed operation based on reliable intelligence. Ideally you should recce the site in person, having studied it first from maps and aerial photographs. The more thorough your preparation and the more complete your rehearsals, the more damage you will inflict on the enemy. My troop sergeant in the SAS used to hammer it in to us: they are ambush *drills*. He would bring us up short of the ambush position and we'd take off our Bergens that would be our cache. We'd move forward into the position, guys dropping off so we were deployed for all-round defence. Everyone worked when that man ambushed, there was nobody sitting about thinking 'This is easy'.

There are two basic types of ambush:

1. Linear ambush

This is used when you know the direction from which the enemy will be approaching. In a deliberate ambush this obviously requires good intelligence of enemy intentions. In an immediate ambush it is because you can see what the enemy is doing. However, in both cases you should still be ready to deal with the sudden approach of the enemy from any direction. Otherwise you are asking to be ambushed yourself.

Linear Ambush
A section ambush can create a killing ground up to 50 metres wide, using a killer group built around a GPMG, with stop groups to either flank and a rear protection group. Claymore mines can obviously be added to sweep the killing ground, but in this case 4 mines have been positioned to protect the ambushers' flanks.

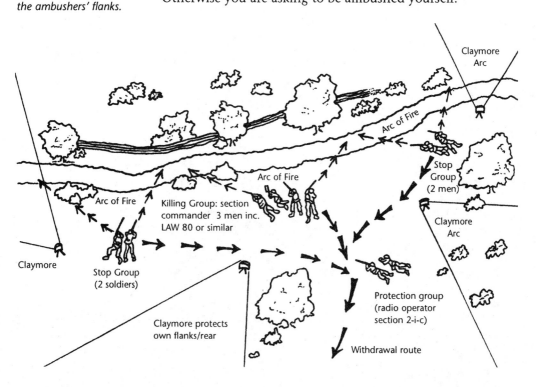

2. Area ambush

This is used where you know the enemy will approach the site, but not from which direction. An area ambush consists of several ambush parties, each lying in wait for the enemy on a given axis. It is more complicated to arrange as it is all too easy to end up firing into each other in the confusion, but when controlled well you can bounce the enemy from one ambush into another. In Vietnam US forces used triangular ambushes, often a reinforced company dug-in in all-round defence in the

Vehicle Ambush
Vehicles are best ambushed just around corners or bridges, rather than on straight roads on which they can speed along. Here the ambush is ready where the vehicles will be travelling slowly. It's also a spot where it will be hard to turn around or drive off the road. The road is cratered to prevent vehicles accelerating and driving their way out. A demolition charge will go off by the bridge the moment the target vehicle has passed it. Cratering the road is one option, but you can also use anti-tank rockets to destroy the first (and ideally the last) vehicles, blocking the road that way.

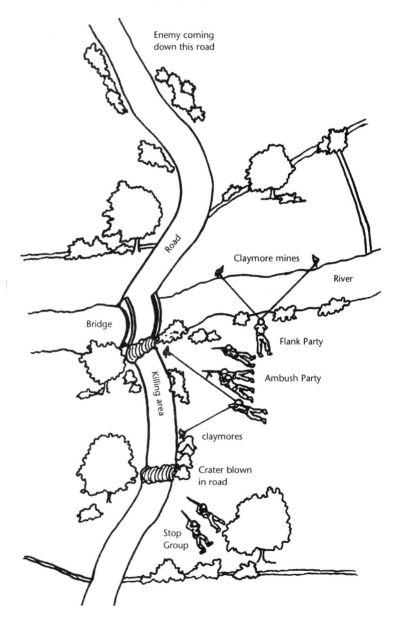

expected path of the enemy. This was necessary because ambushing the NVA could be like grabbing a tiger by the tail: well-trained Vietnamese troops would attempt to flank the position and put in a counter-attack. Vietnam also saw the first widespread use of 'automatic' ambushes: a succession of claymore mines and other anti-personnel devices arranged with interlocking killing zones across the predicted path of enemy forces. Both sides used them, often in conjunction with manned ambushes. The ambush party would make its retreat, sometimes drawing pursuing enemy soldiers into the booby-trapped/mined area. US special forces also rigged groups of enemy dead with grenade traps and claymores to kill enemy casualty clearing parties.

Setting a deliberate ambush

A deliberate ambush might be set and triggered within a few hours, or it might be a long-term operation, taking place at the end of several days' patrolling. It could be conducted by a patrol operating deep behind enemy lines and supported by a patrol base in the same way as the recce missions discussed earlier.

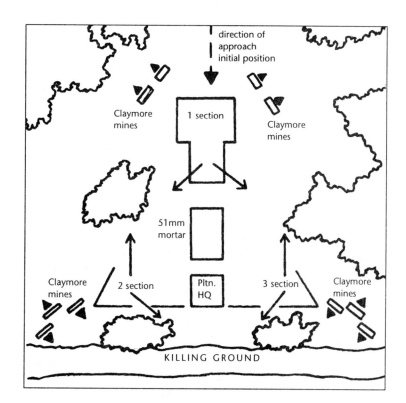

Triangular ambush
This assumes that the enemy is going to be passing along the track. The platoon occupies an all round position of defence while the ambush position is scouted, then occupies a triangular position: one section will carry out the ambush while the others protect its flanks and rear. Claymore mines are used to increase the firepower delivered into the killing ground and also to sweep all approaches to the ambush position.

McALEESE'S FIGHTING MANUAL

The following are typical sites for a deliberate ambush:

- known routes in regular use by the enemy, e.g. roads, tracks, railways
- enemy admin sites like supply/water points, equipment caches
- places where the vegetation changes, e.g. the edge of a wood
- prominently marked places on the map, e.g. bridges, corners of woods, road junctions; basically 'choke points' or likely sites for a rendezvous
- the approach to your own defensive positions
- the approaches to villages (especially in counter-insurgency operations)
- the withdrawal route from your ambush site – be prepared to ambush any pursuing enemy if the force you ambush turns out to be larger than you bargained for

If you have to lie in wait for more than one night, you will need to divide your men into two groups – one manning the ambush and the other resting. Again, as in OP work, you have

'T' shape ambush
This is another way of covering the ambush party with the rest of the platoon. The distances between the sections, HQ and mortar team depend on the ground and whether you are ambushing by day or by night. The ambush assumes the enemy is most likely to be passing along the track, but you have plenty of firepower in all directions in case they are not so obliging.

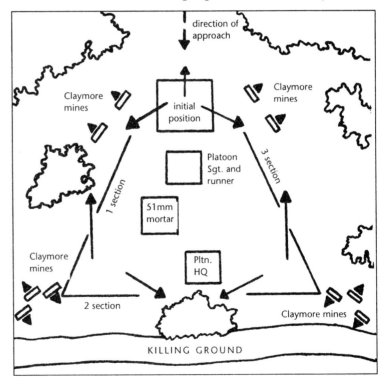

to stay switched on for hour after boring hour, watching your arcs and not relaxing. If an ambush party dozes on the job, the 'hunter' will soon become the 'hunted'. Individual discipline is vital:

- your move to the ambush site must be quiet and unobserved
- keep noise and movement to a minimum
- no coughing, snoring, scratching or farting
- no smoking
- no cooking so have enough cold rations and high-energy food to keep going
- have all weapons ready to fire at a split-second's notice
- make sure everyone knows the signal for opening fire

In the Rhodesian SAS we used to put in a four-man vehicle ambush along a road, with another one maybe a kilometre or two further along the road. Two of you sat in an OP by the road, the other two behind you in what was your administration area. We had a command-detonated mine under the road and RPG7s. One man was on stag, while the others rested or attended to their admin. It was a real gentleman's ambush although we were always pushed for manpower in the SAS. If the enemy convoy proved too big, the idea was to stop just the first two or three vehicles, block up the road and then get the aircraft in to do the business on the rest of the convoy. The ambush could also double as an OP: you let the convoy past but radioed back to HQ and aircraft were scrambled. That way the enemy would not know of our presence on the ground. One of our ambushes stopped an eighteen-vehicle convoy in just this way; we blew up the first truck, and the enemy thought it was just another ambush. They started to manoeuvre against the patrol, which pulled back quickly having already alerted the air force. The aircraft were already on standby and within about fifteen minutes two Hunters came over and took out the convoy.

The ambush party is typically sub-divided into a number of teams. The killer group is tasked with executing the ambush. The flank protection group(s) give early warning of the enemy's approach and guard against an enemy attack from the flank, and can also serve to block the escape of survivors from the killing ground. The rear protection group guards the killer group's back and occupies an RV to which the killer and flank parties will withdraw. This group might also guard

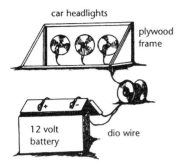

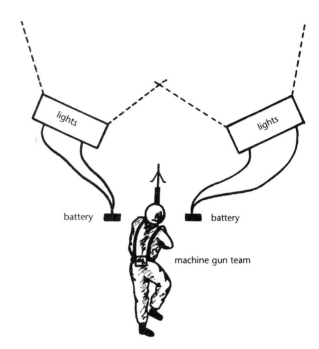

A simple improvisation that can really bathe the ambush area in light is to use banks of vehicle headlights fitted to a simple frame, and powered by a 12 volt battery. You need to think very carefully about carrying heavy, bulky gear to an ambush site, but they can be very effective. Make sure you site the lights so that fire directed at them will miss your position.

everyone's Bergens so the other parties can fight unencumbered, in belt order alone.

Move into position after a thorough recce and rehearsals *by day and night* and check and test all weapons, communications and night illumination. You enter in almost reverse order, with a scout leading, followed by the rear protection party, then the ambush commander then the two flank protection groups. When the flanks and rear are secured, the killer group moves into place. Now halt for a few minutes; watch and listen for the enemy.

You are at your most vulnerable while preparing the ambush. So work quietly. Dig in if necessary and camouflage your positions. Deploy claymore mines both to sweep the killing ground and for flank protection. For a night ambush, use trip-flares or command illumination such as ambush lights. These can be created using car lamps and twelve-volt batteries, but do not put them on your position as they will attract enemy fire. I prefer to keep all my night illumination electrically initiated. The problem with trip-wires is that they get set off by animals or even a strong gust of wind. With electrical initiation you are in control – there's light when you want it and not before.

If you are able to carry lots of kit, five-gallon fuel drums ini-

TACTICS

Setting up a Claymore
Claymores are issued in a bandolier type bag with instructions included. It is designed to be electrically detonated, but I prefer to use det cord to initiate a number of mines together. It is more reliable, especially if the mine is set up some distance away and is part of a series: the danger of a long line of electrically-detonated Claymores is that there might not be enough power in the system to fire the last ones in the series.

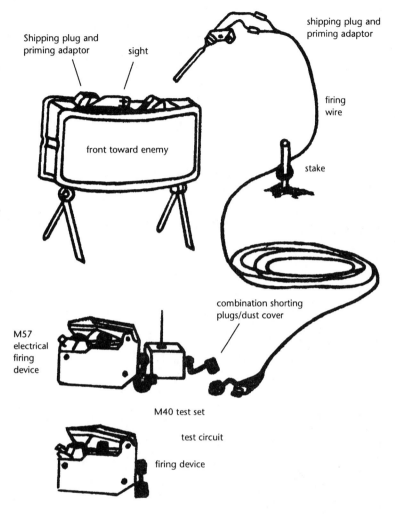

tiated with plastic explosive or *fougasse* improvised claymore-type combinations of explosive and scrap metal can be used to provide an 'anvil' on to which the enemy is driven by the 'hammer' of the killer group. You can string razor wire at ankle height among long grass, between pickets or trees, either to slow an enemy assault on your position or to hamper escape from the killing zone. But these are trimmings really; you probably won't be able to carry all the extra weight. You can do enough damage with RPGs or LAWs plus claymores.

According to the manual, once the work phase is over, the ambush commander should move around the groups and whisper 'ambush set' to everyone. My troop sergeant in the SAS didn't do that. He'd come along and put his hand on your

Aiming a claymore
A claymore mine is a curved plastic case containing 600 steel ball bearings with a layer of C4 plastic explosive behind them. When the explosive is detonated, the ball bearings are blown forward across a 60-degree arc. It is like a gigantic shotgun blast, sweeping everything away up to about 50 metres and still moderately effective at up to 100m. A small team of men with claymores can inflict very disproportionate losses on a larger enemy force.

CLAYMORES
Killing Zones (right)
For best results, position Claymores so that their killing zones overlap.

Claymore mines (left)
Even the 'friendly' side of the mine can be dangerous: at up to 100m behind the Claymore you should be in cover and you must be at least 16m away from it when it goes off. Although the blast of ball bearings is concentrated across the 60 degree arc, there is always some stray fragmentation at up to 90 degrees.

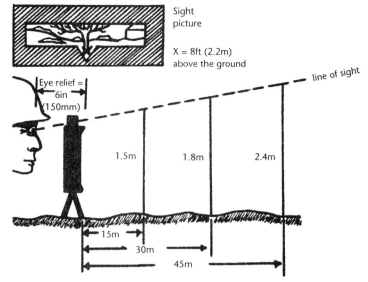

Sight on a point 8ft high, 50 yards away.

shoulder. You'd go, 'Yeah,' and he'd move on to the next guy. He'd make sure he touched every man's shoulder to indicate the ambush was set. Whispering at night-time is risky: your man can confuse it with something else or someone might not get the message. I knew a man who lost his life because of this.

From the moment the ambush is set safety catches are off, grenades are ready to throw and everyone is watching his arcs over his sights and is ready to fire. The commander takes his position with the killer group. There should be no movement on your position.

Don't start an ambush by shouting out 'Now!' or firing a flare or a shot in the air. The slightest pause between the order and the ambush starting could give the enemy time to react. Start an ambush with an aimed burst from your own gun or from a machine gun under your control. Other good openers include setting off a command-detonated claymore.

Two problems can occur as you wait to spring the ambush: civilians wander into the position, or a friendly patrol appears

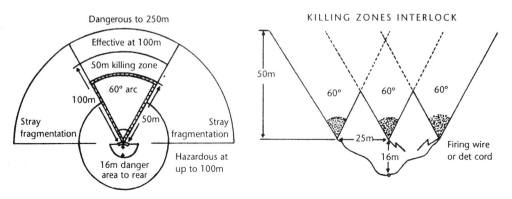

where the enemy is supposed to be. In counter-insurgency operations, the civilians might of course be enemy guerrillas or local people recruited or coerced into serving as guides or porters. You must weigh up the life of the civilian against the lives of your men. Now you can either let the guy go, as McNab did when the kid bubbled him and his patrol (starting the chain of events that led to the patrol being hunted down), or take him prisoner. In the Rhodesian SAS we once did a long-term ambush inside Mozambique, trying to get Josh Ntonugara. What you did with a civilian who blundered into the ambush was cuff and gag him, and if that wasn't enough you'd pump some morphine into him to keep him quiet until you'd done what you were going to do, especially if your target was due to arrive at a certain time.

The third option is to murder the civilian. A lot of people don't have the attitude for this. As Andy McNab said, 'We're the SAS not the SS.' On the other hand the Rhodesians were terrible for it. If someone walked into a Rhodesian ambush, often as not they'd take them round the back and top them with a silenced pistol. On a long ambush you'd end up with a heap of dead bodies at the back of the ambush position. But what you've got to remember is that if you top a person, they're not going to go home that night. If he's from a nearby village, people are going to come and look for him. So you'll attract more people. You might as well wind your ambush up and lift it somewhere else.

I've never been in the business of murdering people; it's unsoldierly and undignified. Again, this is an issue that should be dealt with during your rehearsals. Don't wait until it happens before you figure out what to do. Think ahead – take extra morphine. With morphine, you're not killing someone, you're buying yourself six hours' time.

There is not space here to discuss every possible situation, but the main point to remember is that you cannot expect soldiers to shoot selectively, to distinguish permissible targets from 'no shoots' in the desperate frenzy of an ambush. This is not a practical pistol competition. The ambush commander must decide to initiate the ambush – and kill whoever is in the killing area – or to call it off. If you think the patrol walking into the area is a friendly one, it is better to allow them to pass without seeing you than to try to make contact and warn them off. They may well take you for the enemy and a 'blue-on-blue' firefight will be the result.

Assuming your ambush works and you now have a heap of

Tripflare and reflector
This is a side view of a widely used means of generating light over the killing ground. Because animals, and even the wind, can set off tripflares at the wrong moment, this group of four flares is command-initiated from the ambush position.

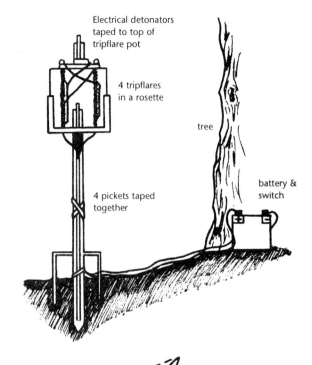

Tripflare with reflector
Tripflares illuminate a circular area, including your position often as not. To restrict them to covering a 180 degree arc pointing in the enemy's direction, rig them with a reflector behind them. Metal lids or cans hammered flat work very well, the Army issue bean tin is a favourite.

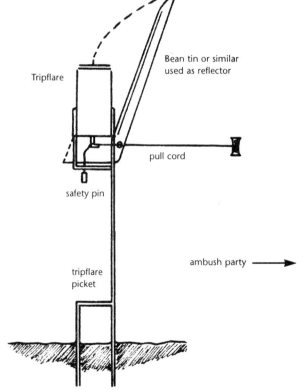

bodies in the killing area, use two-man teams to search the enemy dead for useful intelligence material. Use two men to check each body, one covering the other so that an enemy shamming can be dealt with before he kills someone. A properly executed ambush is intended to kill, not to capture. While it is worth having hoods and plasticuffs handy just in case there are survivors wishing to surrender, I prefer to go through the killing zone topping everyone as you go by – with head shots – double-check the bodies and then proceed to collect documents, intelligence etc. This is the task of the patrol commander, while the second in charge takes command of the perimeter.

On the other hand, you may find yourself having to withdraw under fire. There may have been more enemy than expected, or something might have gone wrong. Your rehearsals should have covered what to do if the killer group has to pull back under fire. Similarly, if the enemy attacks from one flank, the flank protection group falls back on the killer group which pivots around to face the new attack. All groups then fall back on the rear protection group and fire and manoeuvre back to the RV.

Reasons for failure are many, but these are the usual problems that result in an ambush going wrong:

- noise from cocking weapons, releasing safety catches etc.
- radios audible from killing area
- poor camouflage discipline
- too much movement on the position
- communications failure between ambush parties
- enemy arriving from unexpected direction or at unexpected time
- weapon stoppages
- fire opened too early before enemy right inside killing zone
- everyone fired at the same target, leaving some enemy unengaged

A good ambush can enable a small group of guys to take out a much larger force. My friend Pete Cole – an ex-1 Para guy – laid on just such an ambush with an eight-man patrol in Zambia. He had a command-detonated mine in the road when along came this pantechnicon full of enemy troops, which stopped just short of the mine. They obviously thought, 'There's something wrong here', and formed up their troops right on the edge of the killing area. They proceeded to sweep the side of the road, but concluded that there was nothing there and got back on the truck. Pete was sitting there the whole time with his finger on the tit. He waited and waited, till they were all back on board. Boom! What people don't realise is that when a mine goes off under a truck, every loose screw, every piece of glass and anything that's lying free turns into a bit of shrapnel. These guys were knackered. Pete told me, 'I was standing there with my pistol, going "bang, bang bang". I wasn't killing those guys, I was executing them.' There were fifty guys on that truck and eight men slaughtered them. I can think of no better example of an ambush. If you plan a thing well and have the discipline to carry it out, you're going to get the results.

Ambush checklist
Where you set your ambush should:
- be hidden from the enemy
- be without an obvious escape route
- offer you a covered approach in and out
- allow early warning of the enemy's approach
- provide all-round protection
- have a good field of fire

Mining roads
Mine-laying on dirt roads is pretty straightforward, but don't make the mistake often made by the guerrillas in Rhodesia. They would mine the road fairly professionally, but the debris from the mine would be tossed only thirty metres away. If you swept along the side of the road, you would find the box it had been carried in and all the various packaging Russian mines come in. So if you are going to mine a road, take a sandbag along to remove the rubbish.

The Rhodesians countered the mine threat with an improvised vehicle known as the Pooki. It was a Volkswagen fitted with big wide tyres and two flaps that came down. The tyres dissipated the weight of the vehicle as it drove along the road. The ground pressure was so light, the operators used to demonstrate it by driving the thing over your hand. Successful little vehicles, the Pookis were driven in front of convoys. The guerrillas' only counter-measure was a mine connected to a wide expanse of chicken wire, set to detonate on the slightest pressure – which meant it could be set off by almost anything.

Mining metalled roads is harder, but by no means impossible. The difficulty is proportional to the road's state of repair: the bumpier the road, the easier it is to conceal a mine. In Rhodesia the guerrillas used to put diesel on the road, rake up the tarmac and leave what looked like nothing more than a diesel stain. The tarmac would loosen and they'd come back, excavate and put a mine in. Anyone regularly using the road would have got used to the diesel stain (assuming they studied the ground that carefully, which is unlikely). One day you'd drive down the road, and bang!

The Rhodesians countered with mine dogs, using labradors trained to sniff out the anti-tank mines. They were pretty good at it, but they used to go up and sit on the mine – a fault in their training. The gooks switched on to this and started putting anti-personnel mines on top of the anti-tank mines.

We used to lay mines ourselves, inside the front-line states supporting the guerrilla movements. You went in at night and lifted up a block of tarmac with a chisel. Put a poncho by the side and place the spoil on that. Gently chamfer the sides of the hole because a steep-sided hole might not get the vehicle's wheel deep enough inside to trigger the mine. Insert the mine, pop back the tarmac surface and remove any spoil on the road. We used to carry a spray can of black paint so we left what looked like a patch in the road.

HOW TO SURVIVE AN AMBUSH

If an enemy has put out a deliberate ambush, he has chosen that ground. He's not looked at it for just two seconds like you have, he's been there and studied the ground and placed his weapons accordingly. You don't have time to ponder what to do. When the firing starts you rely on anti-ambush drills – instant offensive action. Well-trained troops who have rehearsed their anti-ambush drills can survive the situation and sometimes turn a potential disaster into a victory. It's got to be 'Enemy left!' and straight in – as quick as that. If you start thinking, 'Well, they could have a machine gun here … should I, shouldn't I, could I, couldn't I', you're dead.

I can assure you that it is unnerving if you're in an ambush position and the enemy comes straight at you. This happened to me in Mozambique once, and they wounded some of our guys which they would never have done if they hadn't charged us. The Gurkhas in Borneo were great at this too, instantly steaming

Anti-Ambush 1

(a)
You have made the classic mistake: no scouts out, using a track and approaching an obvious focal point, in this case a bridge over a stream. The enemy ambushes you. Unless you are bullet-proof or they are terrible shots, you have to react instantly to stand any chance of surviving this one.

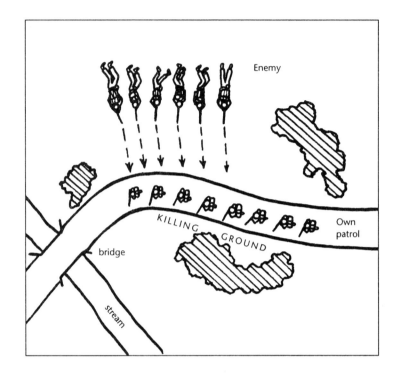

(b)
The North Vietnamese tended to carry B40/RPG2 rockets for just this case: if ambushed, they would immediately fire a volley of anti-tank rockets into the enemy ambush position. You need to counter-attack immediately, deliver as much fire as you can and get in among them. Maximum firepower and maximum aggression are the only ways to survive in this situation.

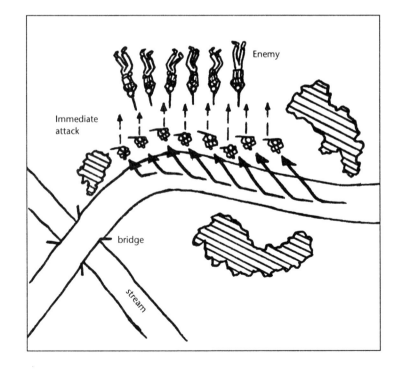

TACTICS

Anti Ambush 2

(a)
Here the main body of the platoon was preceeded by a fire team scouting ahead. The enemy ambush the scouts, who fall back from the killing ground. The rest of the platoon swings around to outflank the enemy ambush party.

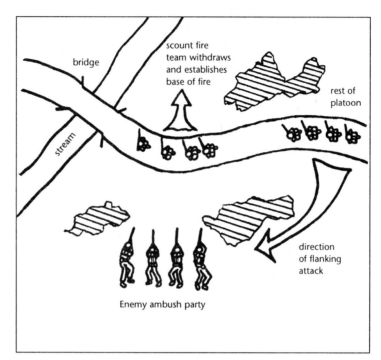

(b)
The Scout team returns fire while the rest of the platoon delivers its attack. Speed is still the key here: you need to get on to the enemy's flank before they can react. Once again: there is no substitute for rehearsals, and what were you doing bimbling down the track in the first place?

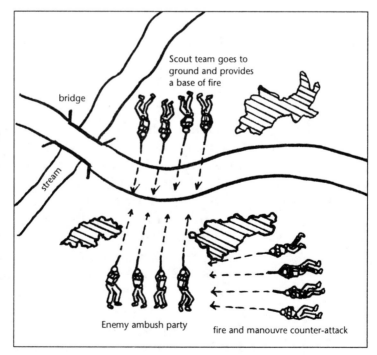

into an enemy ambush and turning the tables on their attackers.

Before we look at anti-ambush drills, it is worth emphasising that it is better to avoid being ambushed in the first place, rather than having to fight your way out of a trap. If you've been soldiering properly, you shouldn't have been caught in an ambush. So avoid routine: do not send out patrols at the same time every day, do not use the same routes if you can avoid it, and stay clear of roads and tracks when you can. If you are moving through the jungle, the only place you can get ambushed is on a track; if you are setting an ambush you aren't going to lie in wait in the middle of the boonies – you will set yourself up on a track, or maybe around a clearing. So don't be tempted to follow the track that happens to be going your way. It is harder to go across country, but safer. Similarly, if you are tracking the enemy, following spoor, don't bimble along in their wake. A switched-on opponent will double back and ambush you. The trick in this situation is to zig-zag, looping back and forth across the track rather than going straight along it.

Thorough reconnaissance is important: check your flanks and scout ahead so that you do not blunder into any nasty surprises. This sounds so obvious, sitting inside in the peace and quiet, but when you are cold and tired and in the middle of nowhere it can be very tempting to cut corners, not to bother patrolling that little wood ahead because you think someone has already checked it. And that's when you get ambushed. Commanders and radio operators are the prime targets in an ambush. If the enemy can kill the commander, control will be lost. So commanders should not wear conspicuous badges of rank, and radio operators should dismount their aerials unless trying to communicate.

Once you are caught in the killing zone it is too late to plan what to do. So rehearse what you would do if ambushed from the left flank, the right flank, both flanks at once, whether by day or night, in open country or thick vegetation. If you are attacked from close range, the best general rule is to attack the ambushers directly. You have to get out of the killing zone as fast as possible, and the enemy will probably expect you to run for it. So attack them without delay, using white phosphorus grenades if you have them – plenty of smoke will add to the confusion. In Vietnam, the North Vietnamese carried shoulder-fired anti-tank rockets (RPG2s and RPG7s) to defend themselves against ambush, firing a volley of rockets into the ambushing forces and following up with an immediate assualt. They knew that with maximum aggression they could turn the tables on their attackers. Of course, this is all very well for a big unit, but not for a four-man patrol. Some Australian SAS patrols in Vietnam converted their FN FAL rifles to fully automatic and removed the flash suppressors from their 5.56mm CAR15s; this enabled a four-man patrol to make an incredible amount of noise as well as to put down a lot of fire. While the Viet Cong were wondering just how big a force they had ambushed, the SAS patrol fired and manoeuvred its way out of the killing zone.

If you are attacked from longer range, you might not be able to overrun the ambushers' positions. In this case, you will have to form a defensive perimeter. Direct your firepower carefully and you might be able to suppress them. You might be able to develop an effective attack or to hold the position until you can call down artillery, air support or even a quick reaction force to help you out. If you do not have any support, then you might have to break out in groups, using fire and manoeuvre to keep your enemies' heads down while you are on the move.

Vehicle ambushes

As the MPLA found out the hard way, if you get ambushed while travelling in unarmoured lorries, your survival time can be measured in seconds. So how do you survive if you don't have the latest cannon-armed armoured personnel carriers and have to rely on an old Unimog to get from A to B? Firstly, prepare the vehicle. The MPLA were sitting in the cab without a single weapon trained on the road ahead. You should:

1. Remove the canopy and its framework and travel with the tailboard down.

2. Put the seats in the middle, so the troops in the back sit facing outwards.

3. Make sure everyone can see and is able to fire his weapon/throw grenades without hindrance.

4. Practise getting out of the vehicle double-quick.

5. Fit towing bars and carry full tool kits so you can clear obstructions and tow damaged vehicles.

6. Avoid overcrowding the vehicles if you can; no more than fourteen or fifteen men in the back of a four-ton truck so you do not get in each other's way.

7. Add sandbags to protect against mines, and any other protection the vehicle loading permits, e.g. grills on the front to help crash through barricades.

8. Add a 7.62mm machine gun mount to each vehicle. Shoulder-fired anti-tank weapons from the 66mm LAW to the 84mm Carl Gustav can also be fired from the vehicle – provided you watch the back blast area. Not only do these tend to put off the enemy ambush party, but you can use them to blow your way through roadblocks. In Rhodesia we used rifle grenades, so the initial response to an ambush was absolutely devastating.

9. If possible, modify the truck like a driving instructor's car with a clutch and brake pedal for the passenger's side as well. That way, if the driver gets hit, you can still drive the vehicle out of danger.

Ideally you should have four men acting as sentries in the back of the truck, covering all angles. If you get ambushed, their job is to lay down automatic fire at the ambushers' positions while everyone else gets out. Another man 'rides shotgun' with the driver. He stays with the vehicle, protecting the driver at all times.

If your convoy of vehicles is ambushed, return fire at once and try to drive on out of the killing zone. Once clear, drivers and 'shotgun' men stay put, the others counter-attack without delay. Warn off any friendly vehicles approaching the ambush area; rather than running the gauntlet, they can halt early and the troops de-bus to attack. If your vehicle cannot drive clear of the killing zone, the sentries engage the enemy position with automatic weapons/anti-tank rockets and plenty of smoke grenades while the rest of the occupants de-bus and assault the ambushers. When you de-bus, run along the tracks of the vehicle if you can. It's the only place you know there aren't any anti-personnel mines, because the truck would have set them off.

It is vital that you know where you are at all times – continuous map reading is essential. Then if you are ambushed, you can summon reinforcements and/or call for artillery or air support. But unless you are on the right square of the right map sheet, you will find yourself on your own.

Defensive battle

It is hard work digging trenches or piling up rocks to create *sangars* – shelters built up from stones when the ground is too rocky to dig in. So make sure you dig them in the right place first time. Defending your position against a reasonably well-equipped enemy means getting under cover; most 'Third World' armies have access to modern artillery and/or aircraft capable of dropping bombs. Many soldiers have come badly unstuck by not taking the enemy artillery threat seriously. The French paras were beaten in Vietnam because their flimsy positions were pounded to bits by Viet Minh artillery. And there has been plenty of film these last few years showing all sorts of heavy artillery in action in the former Yugoslavia. Dig in – or die.

Two types of weapon have priority when you choose your ground for a defensive battle: your anti-tank weapons and your machine guns. Unless you are in dense forest or jungle, defending yourself against tanks is absolutely fundamental and we will be looking at this in more detail soon. Whatever you are equipped with, from 66mm LAW to RPG7, RPG16, LAW80 or even MILAN or similar wire-guided missiles, you need to position them so that they are sheltered from direct enemy fire. Avoid the forward slope of a hill where the enemy might be able to sit back out of range of your weapons and shell you to oblivion. Ideally, you want them to come over a

Reveting
Trenches dug in sandy or loose soils tend to collapse easily, especially when artillery rounds land nearby. Even in heavy soil, trenches are vulnerable under bombardment. To make it as strong as possible, revet the sides with whatever is at hand: here the foxhole is reveted with intertwined branches, but doors, wriggly tin, boards or logs can all play their part. Hammer stakes into the floor of the position to anchor the supports against the side. Hammer more stakes into the surrounding surface and secure the whole thing with cord.

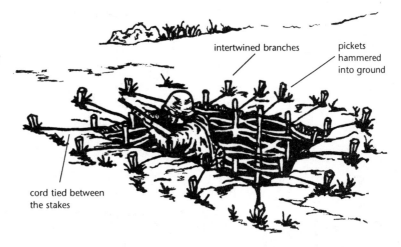

hill crest or round a corner and straight into the effective range of your weapons. Work out which bits of ground are absolutely vital for you to hold – those areas which, if captured by the enemy, would force you to withdraw. You usually find that there is more ground to be occupied than you have men to defend it, so you must prioritise ruthlessly. Avoid the temptation to spread out into a thin line which can easily be broken through or rolled up from either side. You need depth to the position, second or third lines from which to counter-attack.

Machine guns are your second priority. Ideally you want pairs of tripod-mounted, belt-fed 7.62mm machine guns sited where each gun position can support the other. Interlocking zones of fire cover both the front and flanks of your position. Since machine gun fire from the flank is more effective than from directly ahead, the best defensive deployment will have guns on the flanks sited to fire into the flank of an enemy coming straight at your position.

Now deploy your riflemen. Two-man foxholes have the disadvantage that if one man is hit, the other usually stops to help him, leaving no one to shoot at the enemy. Sticking a whole squad or section together requires a big trench which is hard to conceal, and it is difficult to apply enough overhead cover. So split into fire teams of four, and dig mutually supporting trenches. Make sure you have actually checked the area thoroughly before you dig in. It has happened, particularly in jungle warfare, that soldiers have been so busy planning where to put their defences that the presence of a concealed enemy OP nearby has gone unobserved! Clear the area first.

Remember that the enemy might not wait until your cunningly sited defences are complete before launching his attack. Sentries must be deployed to give warning of the enemy's approach while everyone else digs in. While preparing its position, each section should have its Bergens down and weapons pointed towards the arcs of fire they will cover when the trenches are dug. So if the enemy does arrive earlier than planned, at least you have your weapons to hand and hopefully at least a shell-scrape to take cover in. Lastly, just before everyone starts with their shovels and spades, have a final check that what you think should be an interlocking field of fire actually is one. Having to re-position a trench once it is dug is not just tiring and annoying, the enemy might not give you time. While three men dig, the fourth should be making two detailed range cards, one for the fire team and one for the platoon commander.

Once the position is completed and camouflaged, routine administration should be as in patrol base. Many manuals tell you to have a track plan and stick to it, on the grounds that if everyone wanders freely around the position the maze of boot tracks will probably be obvious from the air, if not the ground. However, a track plan can be a terrible giveaway too, especially from the air. Provided you don't have too much movement on the position, and you take care not to disturb your camouflage, you are probably better off without a track plan.

If the enemy still has not put in an appearance, add some dummy positions by digging down a foot or so; camouflaged like the rest of your trenches they will look just like the real thing on an aerial photograph. If you are facing an enemy equipped with infra-red detection kit (and remember that even in the Falklands, the Argentines had better night-fighting equipment than the British), it is worth adding another form of 'dummy' position. IR detectors can be spoofed by old paraffin heaters or just bunches of candles burning in an old ammo tin. This doesn't fool image intensifiers, but any little trick that diverts enemy fire away from your real location has to be worth while.

Defensive position checklist
1. Ground
Site your defences on ground that dominates the surrounding terrain. If your defensive position is overlooked by higher ground, you are not in a defensive position.

2. Depth
A single line of trenches facing the enemy is useless; you need several successive lines of positions so that the rear ones are out of the enemy's sight. You can rally on them and launch a counter-attack from them.

3. Arcs of fire
Site trenches so that you can engage the enemy at the maximum *effective* range of your weapons. No point letting them get any closer than you need them. And make sure arcs of fire interlock, so the loss of a single trench does not create a 'blind spot' through which the enemy can attack.

The 4-man battle trench

This step-by-step sequence shows how to build a battle trench (with overhead cover) for a 4-man fire-team. It involves a lot of hard work, so make sure you've sited it correctly before you start digging. If it seems too much trouble, take a look at a book on World War I and see what artillery can do to people, even when relatively well dug-in. This is the only chance you will have to survive a proper artillery preparation in any state to put up a fight against the enemy infantry.

(a) Mark out the area to be excavated. The exact size of the trench will depend on the number of men in the fireteam, and what they are armed with. The British Army battle trench includes a 4.8m wide section with overhead cover, with 1.8m of open trench at either end. By cutting the turfs and rolling them back as shown, you can dump the spoil from the trench and roll back the turf on top, thus avoiding the telltale heap of earth that identifies your position to the enemy.

(b) Overlapping sheets of corrugated iron ('wriggly tin') serve to revet the trench. Bend them to shape with angle iron pickets and a sledgehammer. The spoil is packed down behind and to the sides of the trench, not in front where it might block your field of fire.

(c) Hammer 6ft (1.8m) iron pickets into the trench to hold the corrugated iron sheets in position. The 'v' side of the picket should face the inside of the trench.

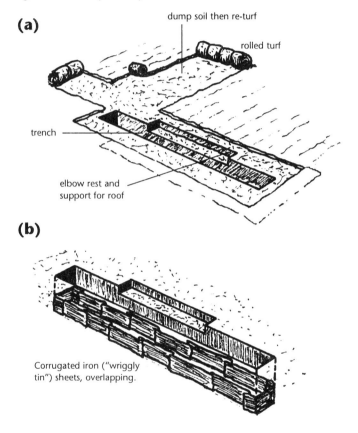

(a) dump soil then re-turf / rolled turf / trench / elbow rest and support for roof

(b) Corrugated iron ("wriggly tin") sheets, overlapping.

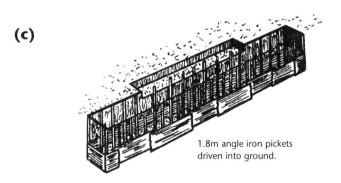

(c) 1.8m angle iron pickets driven into ground.

TACTICS

(d) To support the angle iron pickets inside the trench, hammer several 3ft pickets into the ground at either end of the trench, as shown. Dig a shallow channel between them and the end pickets in the trench and stretch wire between them. Windlass the wire until it is taut and make sure you have done at least four pickets like this. Now the trench should withstand anything short of a direct hit.

(e) The overhead cover will rest on more sheets of wriggly tin, supported by a framework of 6ft iron pickets. Build up ten pillars made from sandbags and rest the pickets on them, thus creating a series of openings that will serve as firing ports.

(f) The complete trench cutaway. You need a bit of open trench to fire most anti-tank rockets as the backblast will take out your own position if you fire from an enclosed position. Remember to leave a sump for water and/or incoming grenades.

(g) The trench as it actually appears. Remember that any vegetation you cut to add to your camouflage will have to be watered and/or replaced to keep it green. This 4-man trench requires 87 6ft pickets, 38 3ft pickets, 244 sandbags, 19kg of heavy duty wire and 36 sheets of corrugated iron. Entrenching even a company on this scale is thus a major engineering task, requiring enormous quantities of kit: hence the importance of using whatever is available locally.

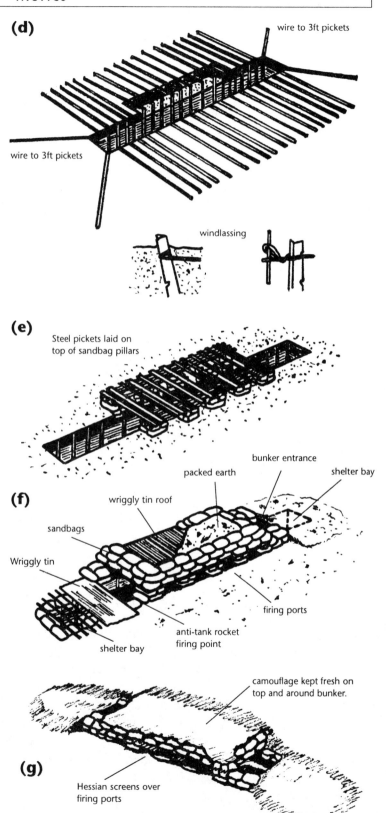

4. Camouflage discipline

All ``positions should be well concealed, and remember to water any plants you have uprooted to cover your trenches. Don't try to hide under the only bit of brown bracken on the hillside. Keep to the track plan and don't leave a trail of boot prints all over the place.

5. Look behind you

It has been known for enemy forces to attack from a direction other than the one from which you were told to expect them! You must be able to observe all around the position to detect an attack from the flank or rear and to be able to deal with it. This means secondary fields of fire, clearly understood, and possibly a few alternate fire positions.

6. Food and water

If you are going to be on the position for any length of time, you have to be able to bring forward supplies without compromising the defences. In the Falklands War, British artillery was called down on Argentine troops who used to come out of their positions to collect food from a truck at the same time every day. Plan how you will supply yourself without enemy interference.

We attacked a town in Angola called Onjuba and we took it from the rear. All the defences pointed towards South Africa, but we went around and drove into it from the north in tanks and armoured cars. We overran the place so fast that we had to go away and re-enact the scene for the cameras, so the South African public got to see the victory. We had to go back, pour petrol over one of the enemy tanks we'd knocked out and set it on fire for the TV crew. Moral of the tale: always prepare for all-round defence.

Communications are usually restricted to radios and whistles when fighting in defence. Runners are easily killed and it is hard to shout loud enough above the noise. However, you must have clear instructions for opening fire. If the enemy has not managed to recce your position carefully and attacks on foot, you want to open fire with every weapon together. Catch them standing up. If a single trench opens fire too early, the enemy will probably hit the deck and drastically reduce the effect of your firepower.

TACTICS

Minefields
Interdiction
Enemy movement can be blocked (interdicted) by the use of nuisance minefields. These can vary from a handful of mines at a crossroads to extensive minefields intended to force large mechanised forces into deploying for action. In full-scale war they can be nourished with mines delivered by aircraft or land-based rockets such as the MLRS system used by many NATO armies. Interdiction minefields can serve to:

1 Disrupt an advance
2 Force the enemy to deploy
3 Draw an enemy on to anti-tank weapons
4 Block access to key areas

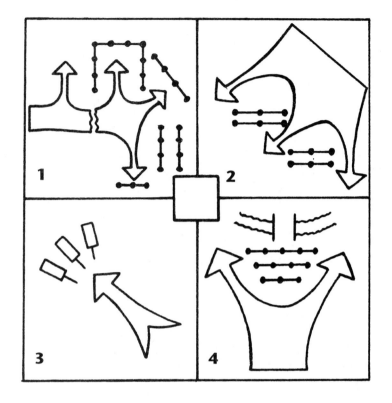

If you have claymores, anti-personnel mines or anti-tank mines, so much the better. But do not think that they will stop the enemy on their own. Mines or obstacles need to be covered by fire to be effective. If they are not, the enemy might find his way through or at least get away without much damage. On the other hand, if you do not have mines you can always add a dummy minefield, marking it off like a real one. A few upturned metal bowls, partially camouflaged, can stop the boldest armoured vehicle commander if he sees them across the track. As the vehicle slows to a halt, shoot the commander as he peers out of the hatch.

Barbed or razor wire can be devastatingly effective, but only if it comes as a surprise; thick belts of wire like something out of World War One can be pounded by enemy artillery or just driven over by a tank. That is what they were originally designed for. If you have wire with which to defend your position, set up an entanglement in long grass where it cannot be seen. It was hidden belts of wire that caused such terrible problems on the Somme. Have a machine gun covering the area so that you can open fire while they are blundering about

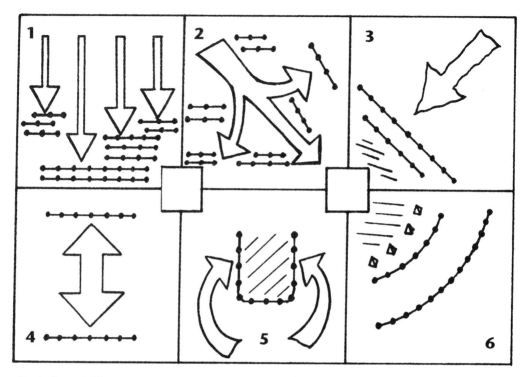

Tactical minefields
Tactical minefields are laid to support your defensive position. They can channel the movement of enemy vehicles, restrict the enemy's freedom of movement or block an advance altogether. Mines delivered by rocket or aircraft can be laid behind the enemy, cutting them off from reinforcements and hampering their withdrawal. The only limits are your imagination and what's left in the quartermaster's stores.
1 Halt or disrupt and attack
2 Ristrict enemy movement
3 Block an advance
4 Stop reinforcement, stop withdrawal
5 Guard your fflanks
6 Strenghtem your defences

trying to find a way through or around. If you put wire directly in front of your trenches, make sure it is far enough away so that the enemy has to get past the wire in order to lob grenades into your trenches.

With good overhead cover, reliable communications and pilots you can trust, you can call down air support to within fifty metres of your own position provided your positions are marked from the air. Helicopter gunships can fire even closer if the enemy looks like overrunning your trenches. But if your artillery and mortars fall silent and the air support never arrives, the final stage of defensive battle begins.

LAST-DITCH DEFENCE

If the enemy manages to fire and manoeuvre forward, hitting your trenches with enough automatic fire to drive you below the parapet, it is only a matter of time before you find a grenade landing at your feet. You have to stop him getting that close. One of the other reasons for having four-man defensive positions is that it is easier to maintain all-round observation than if there are just two of you in a foxhole. And you have to keep a good look-out even when the enemy is attacking from the front. It is very easy to get carried away, exchanging fire with the enemy in front of you and not noticing a couple more enemy soldiers quietly sneaking around the side.

Although a narrow trench provides better cover against shell splinters than a wide one, a true slit trench makes it impossible for you to lob grenades at your attackers. So build in a wider bay to your fire position from which you can start lobbing grenades if the enemy gets that close. And if you cannot stop him there, it is time to get out and fight in the open. Don't make the fatal error of staying in the trench to the very last moment. Once the enemy is able to get close enough to post a grenade through the firing slit of your bunker, or over the lip of your trench, you have had it.

MEN AGAINST TANKS

Tanks are continuing to get bigger and heavier. The American M1 Abrams, the German Leopard 2 and the British Challenger all weigh over fifty-five tons, and the latest Russian design, the T94, is almost as heavy. They carry an enormous amount of armour to protect themselves against anti-tank missiles, and reactive armour – pioneered by the Israelis and Soviets – gives them even better defence against shoulder-fired infantry anti-tank weapons. However, the price of the very latest tanks is so high that you are unlikely to find yourself fighting against them. Only the main NATO powers are likely to be operating them. Across the rest of the world for at least the next decade or so, you are likely to face the older generations of main battle tank: T54s, T62s, T72s etc. Many smaller armies also rely more on wheeled armoured vehicles with low-recoil 105mm guns or similar, a 'poor man's tank'. Both older tanks and newer light vehicles are vulnerable to the sort of portable anti-tank weapons you are likely to be using.

Attacking tanks – even older ones operated by second-division armies – is no easy business. Unless you are well equipped with the latest anti-tank guided weapons, like MILAN or TOW, you need to catch the tanks where they cannot exploit the long range of their weapons and their greater speed. Ambush them on roads or tracks where they cannot manoeuvre easily off the highway.

Even the latest generation of tanks is vulnerable to attack from the sides and rear by shoulder-fired anti-tank weapons. Site your ambush to engage them from the flank after you have slowed or stopped the enemy's advance. And for Western soldiers used only to Western weapons: if you find yourself using Soviet anti-tank rockets like the RPG7, note that they are aimed differently if there is a cross-wind. Whereas you aim off in the direction from which the wind is blowing when shooting a rifle, you aim in the same direction as the wind when aiming an RPG7. This is because it has a set of fins that pop out when it is fired; these will catch the wind and turn the missile. Thus, if the wind is blowing from the right, aim a little to the left of the target.

The best way to halt the enemy is to blow up the leading vehicle with a mine. The British Mk7 anti-tank mine is typical of the sort in widespread service today. Weighing 14.5kg (32lb), it contains 9kg (20lb) of explosive and will blow the tracks of the best protected tanks in the world. Its double-impulse fuse allows men to tread on it without danger and it is not fooled by mine-roller devices sometimes attached to the front of a tank. It will allow the roller to pass over before detonating below the tank.

Smaller mines are easier to carry and most modern ones are made largely of plastic, making them almost impossible to find with a metal detector. If you have to mine a wider area, the British bar mine is a useful bit of kit. At a length of 1.2 metres it has much the same effect but the vehicle is more likely to detonate it. Off-route mines can be sited to fire shaped charges into the sides of enemy vehicles. These are best command-detonated once the ambush begins, but they can be initiated by a wire which the vehicle passes over. The big advantage of these is that you can hang them in trees or off buildings to attack the vulnerable tops of armoured vehicles. Claymore mines are also well worth bringing to a tank

As Soviet tank crew discovered in Grozny, determined men on foot can get close enough to knock out even the latest armoured vehicles. In built-up areas, tanks have to be closely supported by infantry to stop this sort of thing happening: so if you are defending, use machine guns and mortar fire to separate the enemy infantry from the armour.

Attack with satchel charge or anti-tank grenades

shoot at sights, vision blocks and optical equipment

TACTICS

Tank crew have a very restricted view once they shut the hatches and rely solely on their vision blocks to see the world around them. It is particularly significant at close ranges: major blind spots occur and turret-mounted weapons cannot engage targets within about 20 metres of the vehicle. This can be exploited by determined infantry equipped with anti-tank grenades, 'Molotov cocktails' or demolition charges.

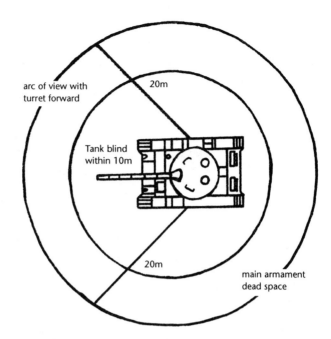

ambush. They can be used as part of the initial detonations to kill anyone sitting up in the turret or to catch enemy infantry as they get out of armoured personnel carriers to counter-attack you. White phosphorus (WP) grenades are also valuable: in daylight they will provide smoke to hamper enemy troops de-bussing from vehicles, and to shield your withdrawal. At night they play havoc with night-vision devices.

Place the mines where the enemy cannot turn around, or mine the obvious turning point as well. Try to find a defile or a point where the road passes between dense vegetation to spring your ambush – and plan your escape route carefully. Use the same routine as you would for ambushing, as outlined above. The difference is that you may be pursued by armoured vehicles (if it goes wrong) so your withdrawal route should ideally be across ground unsuitable for armour. If time permits, you should dig in your ambush position; immobilising a tank by blowing off its track does not stop determined tank crew from firing back with everything they have. That is how Audie Murphy became

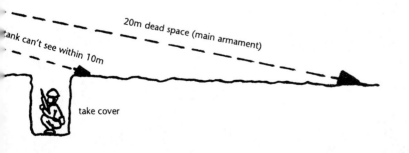

the most highly decorated American soldier in World War Two.

A tank ambush must be prepared to deal with enemy infantry attacking. In Afghanistan, the Russians lost so many tanks to *mujahedin* ambushers with RPG7s, they made sure every tank in a vehicle convoy was accompanied by a dedicated squad of infantry. The foot soldiers put in an aggressive counter-attack the moment the Afghans sprang the ambush, with supporting fire from anti-aircraft cannon mounted on army lorries. Your ambush plan should be ready to give enemy infantry a hot reception from claymores, anti-personnel mines and machine guns.

Nuclear, biological and chemical warfare (NBC)

The continuing controversy over Gulf War syndrome highlights our lack of knowledge about chemical warfare. One theory about its cause is that the combination of antidotes injected as a defence against possible chemical attack is itself harmful, especially when used for long periods. Iraq has used chemical weapons many times in the 1980s, dropping poison gas – or, to be more specific, the nerve agent sarin – on Kurdish towns, killing thousands of men, women and children.

Biological weapons are basically diseases, some naturally occurring but modified to make them more infectious and/or lethal. Since they pose almost as much threat to whoever uses them, their use has generally been away from the battlefield. For instance, during World War One German agents infected Argentine livestock with anthrax and other diseases, killing horses and other animals being shipped to Britain. The Japanese used anthrax in China, but managed to kill several thousand of their own soldiers who advanced into the area unaware of the danger.

Chemical weapons are the poor man's nuclear weapon, and you must be prepared to deal with them. Actual nuclear weapons are rather less likely to be encountered, but with the collapse of the old Soviet Army all sorts of weapons are getting into the wrong hands. And you do not need anything like as much weapons-grade plutonium to build nuclear warheads as was originally thought. So wherever you are fighting, you need to make a careful assessment of the NBC threat and take appropriate action.

NUCLEAR THREAT

Nowadays, the threat comes less from the 'Dr Strangelove' world of intercontinental ballistic missiles than from small atomic weapons that could be obtained by almost any country in the world prepared to pay for them. The Soviet Army had tens of thousands of 'tactical' nuclear weapons and you might very well face an enemy army with nuclear-tipped 'Scud' type rockets or sub-kiloton bombs delivered by aircraft. Without proper NBC defensive equipment, you have little defence against them. Your protection lies in avoiding becoming a target; good camouflage discipline and a high standard of security are required. In this situation the enemy probably does not have too many nuclear weapons and will only expend them on high-value targets.

Keep dispersed and keep dug in. If you are caught in the open with no cover available, lie down with your feet towards the explosion and keep your eyes shut. It is worth remembering that the sort of radiation produced by atomic weapons is halved by a metre of well-packed earth or 600mm of brick. Take whatever shelter is available and cover all exposed skin. If you are in a building, shut all doors and windows to stop fall-out from penetrating. Sealed rations should be edible as they are resistant to contamination, but dairy products are easily contaminated. Use water from underground wells rather than surface sources and do not drink from unprotected water sources within forty-eight hours of a nuclear detonation. Water-purifying kits have no effect on residual radiation.

If you are equipped with NBC protective clothing, take the drills seriously and be ready to use it. If an explosion takes place, wait for the immediate effects to pass and then report the bearing of the cloud and its estimated range. That way all neighbouring units will have some warning of the fall-out. Keep a radio switched off and wrapped in tin foil (if, as is likely, there is no lead available). A nuclear explosion produces an electro-magnetic pulse that will damage all nearby radio equipment. Once there has been an explosion, keep your respirator on at all times and remember to change the filter when necessary. Decontaminate thoroughly – your life depends on it.

CHEMICAL THREAT

If there is a threat that the enemy might employ chemical weapons, you have to treat every attack as a possible chemical one. Assume that a chemical attack is occurring:

- if you are bombarded by artillery, mortars, rockets etc.
- you detect low-flying aircraft
- you observe suspicious smoke, droplets, or mist

- you smell something unusual
- you or anyone else experience typical symptoms of chemical poisoning, e.g. dim vision, stinging eyes, sudden headache, tightness in the chest, running nose, or excess saliva in the mouth
- someone sounds the alarm

The Immediate Action drill will vary depending on which type of NBC equipment you are using, but the basics are the same. The main point is that you must be so well practised you can get the kit on quickly without errors. The Soviet Army used to use real chemical agents on some exercises, accepting that some soldiers would be killed as the price for getting the others to learn the drill properly. In real war, there is no re-test.

The Immediate Action (IA) drill for chemical attack is to kneel with your back to the wind, hold your breath and close your eyes. Take off your helmet and get out your respirator. When you put it on, don't pull it down over your face in case you have droplets of poison on your head; stick your face into the mask, chin first. Don't take a 'last breath' before putting on the respirator – you might get a mouthful of sarin. And one is all it takes.

With your respirator safely secured, blow out hard and shout 'Gas! Gas! Gas!' Check that you don't have any hair sticking between the mask and your face. This would break the seal and leave you exposed to contamination. Put up your hood, decontaminate your hands, put on your gloves and get out your detector paper. Once under cover, carry out your decontamination drills.

2 THEATRES OF WAR

Fighting in the desert

Before the Gulf War few people thought the British Army would ever again have to fight in a desert. The fact that 1944-pattern desert smocks were issued in 1991 suggests this view was certainly shared by the quartermasters. More alarming was the comment from several SAS officers that we had lost the skills we learned fifty years ago in North Africa. Today, the Middle East is still highly volatile, Algeria has a civil war and there are conflicts throughout the Sahara and former Soviet central Asia. Desert operations are back on the agenda.

The trouble is, in these days of 'rapid deployment' you could find yourself out in the sand within forty-eight hours of getting on a transport aircraft, ready to fight someone who has lived in the desert all his life. It is a very different environment, and it demands understanding.

The military attitude to deserts has been described as 'the tactician's dream but the quartermaster's nightmare'. The lack of trees, towns and rivers mean there are fewer limits on where you can move, but every silver lining has a cloud. Vehicles consume a lot more fuel, men have to have water and the heat plays havoc with all sorts of military equipment. Circumstances might not allow it, but you should do everything possible to get acclimatised before going into action. It takes at least a fortnight to adjust to the bizarre combination of blistering hot daytime temperatures and often freezing cold nights. A good suntan helps protect your skin, but do not strip down to your shorts the moment you arrive – this is a lesson you should have learned on holiday. En route to the Falklands, the Parachute Regiment had to make it an offence to get sunburn as so many soldiers were burning themselves on the decks of the *Canberra* as the Task Force sailed towards the Equator.

And remember the other lesson from beach holidays: just because the sun goes in behind a cloud does not mean it can't still burn you. So stay clothed, wearing loose uniforms, and drink small amounts of water at frequent intervals rather than gulping down masses all at once. Do not try to 'ration' water, even the Israelis have had to abandon the idea that you can make yourself do with less water with regular practice. But do not waste it either. Three quarters of your body weight is actually water and you only have to lose 2.5 per cent of it through dehydration to sharply reduce your stamina. A loss of 15 per cent will kill you. Military operations in the desert have often been dictated by the availability of water. One man doing heavy work, like digging in, might need twenty-five pints of water a day. Multiply for a platoon or company and you see the size of the problem if you are at some distance from a water source. Even if you are doing nothing, you can lose up to a pint of water an hour through sweating alone. Four hours of sitting still in the heat without a drink will lose you the 2.5 per cent just mentioned.

Sustained sweating will also reduce the amount of salt in your body, so if you are consuming more than a gallon of water a day, you will need salt tablets to compensate. Dissolve them in water and drink them, rather than swallowing them like a pill. Look out for vegetation that indicates the presence of water. Some plants like cactus store water and they could be growing a long way from any water, but palm trees need water within about a metre of the surface. Cottonwood and willow trees need water within about four metres of the surface. In Angola we used to carry lengths of rubber tubing so we could siphon up water that was too deep to reach with a cup. It could double as a tourniquet too. Study the desert environment in which you will be fighting and discover the likely sources of water.

Lose no opportunity to maximise your water supply. When I jumped with the South African Paras in Angola and southwest Africa, I made the guys bring containers of water to drink on the drop zone before commencing operations. That way they replenished the water they had lost through sweating in the aeroplane without recourse to their water bottles. They started operations on the ground carrying their full supply of water. Another South African idea was to fill the bottom of the mine-resistant APC, the Buffel, with water. It provided a life-saving cushion against mine blast but also doubled as an emergency water reserve.

The wind in the desert has no moisture in it and it has a drying effect on your eyes, mouth and skin. Keep covered up – this is why desert peoples wear various types of head-dress. A good set of goggles is essential.

And find out what the temperatures are actually like. Do not repeat the Gulf War SAS patrol disasters which saw men dying of hypothermia in the freezing conditions typically encountered in winter in north-west Iraq. In other deserts in other seasons, it is not the absolute temperature that is dangerous, but the massive drop in temperature during the night. I can remember having to wear the old heavy army greatcoat in an open-air cinema in Aden. The temperature that night was no lower than sixty degrees Fahrenheit, but it had been well over 100 degrees in the afternoon.

Use the minimum amount of lubrication on all weapons. Oil attacts sand and a well-oiled rifle will have repeated stoppages as a result. Cover the muzzle and ejection port of your rifle to keep out grit and sand. If you have a choice of weapons for the environment (sometimes the mercenaries' prerogative), something that fires every time is better than something wonderfully accurate on the target range but prone to jam in harsh conditions. Also, in desert conditions you can often engage at much longer ranges. Fashionable 5.56mm rifles are completely out-ranged by 7.62mm weapons, as the Omanis have found in recent years. In Somalia, some unfortunate US Army Rangers found themselves losing a firefight with the locals because their MP5 9mm sub-machine guns were hopelessly out-ranged by the Somalis' Kalashnikovs and heavy machine guns.

Vehicle windshields need covering when not on the move as the sand will damage them very quickly. They also reflect the sun, betraying your position for miles. Since digging in is often impossible, camouflage netting and cloth are essential. Exploit the dramatic contrast between light and shadow to break up the familiar shape of vehicles or equipment. But remember that shadows will move during the course of the day and what works in the morning might be a dead giveaway by the afternoon. The US Army has a purpose-built mesh screen that blocks infra-red emissions, matching itself to almost any terrain. You will probably have to make do with wire-mesh camouflage netting with strips of cloth or hessian attached. It will break up shapes nicely and casts irregular shadows, so long as it slopes very gently when placed over a vehicle or position. When I was serving with the Parachute Regiment in Bahrain we used to carry four sticks and some hessian – that's what you used to keep the sun off you.

Visibility is affected by the very strong light; the combination of bright sunshine and unlimited visibility makes it easy to underestimate distances. This is particularly obvious in the early morning and late afternoon when you will usually have the best visibility in the cooler air. The middle part of the day often produces mirage conditions, and in any case, the heat shimmer from the desert floor can sharply reduce visibility. This makes high ground very important; unless elevated a few metres from the deck, anti-tank guided missiles cannot exploit their full range. You could find yourself engaged by enemy tanks while your own missiles are unable to see the target properly. Also, at ground level you are most vulnerable to the traditional desert warriors' trick of attacking near dawn or dusk, when the sun is low and behind them. Defenders find themselves unable to sight their weapons properly as they have to look right at the sun.

If you are deployed to the desert so quickly that your vehicles are still an unhelpful shade of factory green, a useful camouflage trick is to smear oil all over the hull. Drive along a bit and the dust will stick everywhere, effectively camouflaging your vehicle.

DESERT SURVIVAL KIT

If you do get cut off from your unit, the desert is often a bigger threat than the enemy. For every World War Two survival story of soldiers drinking urine and/or water from radiators of wrecked vehicles as they marched back to British lines, there are many who simply disappeared. Keep the following items with you, and practise with them regularly. Don't wait to learn fire-lighting skills until you are in a situation where your life depends on them! The kit list:

- whistle
- panel of fluorescent material to signal to aircraft
- ground-to-air recognition tables and Morse code sheet
- heliograph
- signal flares
- small container of salt
- torch
- dextrose tablets
- flint and steel

- spare compass (button type)
- waterproof matches
- several small candles
- strong needle and thread
- cotton wool for use as tinder
- condom for water carrying
- wire saw with loop-type handles
- water-sterilising tablets

Fighting in the jungle

I went to Borneo in February 1965 as a young trooper in D Squadron, SAS. I quickly learned that jungle operations are relentless hard work. The conditions of patrolling secretly in the jungle imposed a very strict code of professionalism on the SAS, and it was here that I learned what the SAS means by strict attention to detail.

We learned how to move through the shadowy green foliage, eat and sleep without leaving sign of our presence, and read the enemy's tracks. We spent hours moving slowly and noiselessly in four-man patrols, learning how to navigate in the forest and testing our skills against each other. For a month we lived under the harsh tactical disciplines of no noise, whispering all the time and living on 'SAS hard routine' with no lights, no smoking and no hot food. We became very lean, very pale from not seeing the sun under the canopy, and very fit.

Since the SAS was re-formed in the 1950s it has spent a great deal of time 'patrolling green', as it calls it. To this day, the regiment trains hard for jungle warfare, operating in four-man patrols for extended periods. Three or four weeks is a long time for a four-man team to keep going, and even with every effort to cut down the weight carried, tremendous loads have to be borne. It demands supreme standards of physical fitness, and even then I lost about a pound of body weight per day on patrol in Borneo. In Malaya we were doing three-month patrols, and some operations in Borneo went on even longer.

Jungles, like deserts, have their own characteristics and you must study the key features of the area in which you find yourself operating. Some are extremely wet, as the US Marines found in the Pacific War on jungle-clad islands which had five metres' annual rainfall. Some are affected by the seasons: Vietnam's forests go through a dry season during which water supply for jungle patrols is a real problem. Patrolling during the dry season can mean carrying 15 to 20kg of water in addition to all your other kit.

'Primary jungle' is the natural state; huge trees up to fifty or sixty metres tall project above a canopy formed by the spreading leaves of smaller ones about half as high. Creepers dangle down to the jungle floor which, because it never sees the sun, is often relatively clear of vegetation. You can pick your way between the massive tree trunks and visibility can be up to fifty metres. 'Secondary jungle' is very different. If man has cleared an area of forest and then abandoned it to nature, vegetation grows up thick and fast. A great mass of shrubs and grasses create a green wall, visibility is cut to a few metres and you might have to cut yourself a path. Tropical grasslands are another nightmare, with sharp-edged grasses standing five or six metres high.

Movement can be terribly slow. Patrolling green, an SAS patrol moves tactically all the time, but this can reduce your movement rate to 100 metres per *hour*. The sheer difficulty of movement in the jungle has to be experienced to be appreciated. The combination of dense vegetation, steep hills and numerous rivers channels movement along predictable paths, making ambushes a favourite tactic. With visibility so restricted, noise discipline is vital. Sounds can carry a long way, and smells too – so no smoking. It is next to impossible to surprise a soldier who is sitting quietly in the jungle, movement tends to be noisy thanks to the vegetation, so frequent listening halts are essential when you are on the move. Good camouflage is equally essential; cake on the cam cream and use one that has an insect repellent incorporated. Camouflage all equipment too and check that your camouflage uniforms are still effective once wet. Many combat uniforms appear almost black when wet, which can betray your position all too easily.

Your quick-reaction drills must be well rehearsed because if you bump into the enemy, you will do so at very short range. In Borneo the SAS planned to 'shoot and scoot', if necessary leaving a wounded man behind. Whether you are tasked with covert recce or something more aggressive, the first few seconds of an encounter in the jungle are often decisive, so see the enemy first and shoot the enemy first.

Navigation is vital in the jungle, especially as the map might not be accurate. Jungle wildernesses are not top priority for cartographers, as the Americans found out in Vietnam. The topographic surveys inherited from the Japanese and French colonial authorities were often out by hundreds of metres. Man-made structures had often moved anyway, and in jungles the world over the local inhabitants move their villages every few years. British operations behind Japanese lines in Burma during World War Two often found villages where none was marked on the map, and nothing but new growth of jungle where the houses were supposed to be. If you are unsure of your position, you are going to impose serious delays on any air or artillery support you might call for.

In Vietnam the US armed forces expended six million tons of bombs and fired some twenty million artillery rounds. But they lost the war. The tremendous firepower available to US forces was able to save many small units from being overrun when they found themselves surrounded by enemy force in the jungle, but it was one thing to save the odd isolated patrol but quite another actually to kill the North Vietnamese or Viet Cong soldiers. Dense jungle can shield you from the heaviest firepower. Aircraft find it difficult to locate targets, even if the air strike is being co-ordinated by a Forward Air Controller (FAC) in a helicopter or light aircraft. If you are fighting an enemy with superior airpower and artillery, the jungle enables you either to melt away undetected or to 'hug' the enemy's own positions, making them unable to fire for fear of hitting their own men. The North Vietnamese used the latter tactic so often that US re bases were prepared with enough overhead protection to allow them to call down fire directly on their own position. Provided the gunners knew their stuff and had variable time fuses ready (producing low air bursts rather than ground detonations) the Viet Cong could be driven off. Such drastic measures are not to be attempted lightly.

The US Army's powerful artillery was only able to strike at the North Vietnamese on the enemy's terms. In the jungle it was almost impossible to be sure of anyone's position, so artillery observers would call down fire at least 1000 metres away from friendly positions. Then they would 'walk' the artillery on to the target, advancing the shells by 100-metre increments. So an alert North Vietnamese commander could either pull out of the area before the artillery landed on target, or launch an immediate attack. Even the US Army, with all its communications equipment, was unable to get artillery fire down in under five minutes if a patrol ran into the enemy. The big 175mm or eight-inch heavy pieces that really did the damage could take twice as long. This problem can only be solved by widespread use of global positioning devices and extensive training, so if you are preparing for jungle operations today, be aware of just how much the terrain will reduce the value of artillery.

Tanks and armoured vehicles are obviously handicapped in the jungle and are often confined to roads and tracks. Road-bound French 'mobile groups' were eventually defeated in their battle for Indo-China, and although modern tanks are far better protected than the World War Two relics they were using, at the close combat ranges of jungle warfare even the latest M1s or Challengers are vulnerable to shoulder-fired anti-tank weapons. They are also far too heavy. Few jungle roads will support a sixty-ton tank, so modern armies preparing for jungle combat tend to buy light tanks or even armoured cars with 105mm guns. However, some areas of jungle are better suited to armoured operations than others, so you cannot assume that tanks will be useless in any and all jungles. In large parts of Vietnam, the US Army achieved great success with heavily armed armoured personnel carriers (APCs). With a .50 calibre machine gun in a cupola and numerous 7.62mm machine guns fitted with shields, these ACAVs (Armored Cavalry Vehicles) proved mobile enough to deal with areas of secondary jungle and even the swamps of the Mekong Delta. Patton's 11th Armored Cavalry even managed to get M48 medium tanks into surprising places, thanks to thorough reconnaissance of the ground. This achieved some remarkable tactical surprises against the Viet Cong who thought themselves safe from tank attack.

GUERRILLA FORCES

Whichever jungle you find yourself fighting in, the odds are that you will be facing a guerrilla army which will avoid a stand-up fight whenever it can, melting back into the jungle when pressed only to re-emerge once the security forces have moved on. Guerrillas are more dependent on political action than firepower and, as has often been demonstrated, sometimes the sheer volume of government firepower plays into the hands of the guerrillas. It is no good defeating a small guerrilla unit if you trash several villages in the process. The guerrillas will then receive more than enough replacements as pissed-off villagers volunteer to fight for them. In most jungle wars since 1945, the struggle for the 'hearts and minds' of the local people has been the ultimate objective of military action. In the SAS I found myself providing medical aid for people (and livestock) at remote forts in Aden. In Rhodesia I saw how the Smith government failed to repeat the British success with 'protected villages' that had defeated the guerrillas in Malaya. On the other hand, the Malayans were getting independence once the guerrillas were beaten.

Since artillery and aerial bombing are so often ineffective in the jungle, and the use of heavy firepower near population centres will have negative political effects, there is no doubt that the best way to defeat the guerrillas is to play them at their own game. Well-trained infantry who are not afraid of the jungle can take the war to the enemy. In Malaya, the British defeated a determined Communist terrorist movement by dividing the guerrillas from the population, preventing recruitment or intimidation. With the population safe in protected villages, the security forces then concentrated on jungle patrolling to locate and destroy the guerrillas. Eventually the guerrillas were driven into the remote jungle highlands, right away from the population centres, and the revolution petered out. The formula must be adapted to particular circumstances, but the system of protected villages and aggressive patrolling has proved to be the only way to defeat insurgents in these parts of the world.

Firefights in the jungle start suddenly and violently and it is easy to 'freeze' for a few seconds – a hesitation that could get you killed. Only frequent rehearsal, with live rounds, will enable you to 'break the spell' when it happens for real. You must have reliable automatic weapons. And you must carry a great deal of ammunition. Just as the Falklands War revised British ideas about how many rounds to carry, so its experience in Vietnam led the Australian SAS to carry 300 5.56mm rounds as standard on a patrol. Belt-fed machine guns are very important, enabling even a small unit to put down a great deal of firepower in a jungle firefight. But look after the ammunition; in tropical conditions, linked ammunition deteriorates rapidly so spray it with a water-displacing spray like WD-40 and carry it in waterproof containers (the Australian SAS cut up lilo mattresses to make plastic sleeves). Inspect the ammunition regularly.

How much ground a patrol can cover depends on the type of jungle. In Borneo, the Commonwealth forces could patrol ten kilometres a day, but against the Viet Cong the Australian SAS found three kilometres a day quite enough for a five-man patrol. Even if the terrain had allowed you to move faster, this was not a wise move given the enemy's high standard of field-craft. Avoid routine at all costs; even the Viet Cong had a habit of stopping around midday for two hours, which could be exploited by enterprising Free World forces.

Most American attempts to win the Vietnam War through superior technology failed to live up to expectations. But the one new system that did deliver enormous results was the use of the helicopter. The 1st Air Cavalry Division inflicted a series of heavy defeats on the North Vietnamese Army using its helicopters to insert blocking forces that trapped enemy units where they could be pounded by artillery and airpower. Helicopters also enabled the Air Cav to reinforce isolated units with surprising speed. Vietnamese attempts to fight back with anti-aircraft guns and by mining likely landing zones were defeated by massive aerial bombardments ahead of helicopter assaults. Helicopter gunships, from the early UH1Bs with machine guns to the purpose-built AH1 Cobra, were able to bring down tremendous volumes of fire with great precision, engaging Vietnamese forces within fifty metres of US troops.

Do not forget that the US withdrawal from south-east Asia was not due to its army being defeated. American voters decided that the preservation of South Vietnam was not worth any more American lives. The jungle is a hard place to fight in, and one that reduces the effect of modern weapons, but it is not an impenetrable shield.

Fighting in the bush

As we stalked through the trees and long dry grass, sweeping the area, a black guerrilla suddenly leapt up right in front of me, no more than a couple of paces away, like a rabbit flushed from the long grass. Stupidly, he turned to run. Instinctively, I lifted my FN to my shoulder and straight away shot him in the back of the head. To my horror, his skull literally exploded.

I have fought in Angola, Namibia, Mozambique, Tanzania and Zimbabwe. The African bush varies from semi-desert to mountainous and there is a dramatic difference between the wet and dry seasons. It is a unique environment in another way: despite years of European influence – whether from western Europe or the Communist bloc in the 1970s and 1980s – African armies are very different. Recruits are drawn from rural peoples, not towns. What they often lack in formal military skills they can make up with their natural understanding of the environment. While the white soldiers of the Selous Scouts were incredibly good, their black scouts were positively uncanny. They had a real sixth sense for where the terrorists were and possessed invaluable local knowledge. For instance, one guy sussed that a village was harbouring terrorists because the same woman went for water four times, far more than he knew she would want unless she had some extra 'guests' with AKs. By the standards of Western recruits, African soldiers are exceptionally fit and can march phenomenal distances. As central and west Africa seem in a state of near permanent anarchy, this is perhaps the most likely theatre of war for UN and possibly NATO soldiers in the late 1990s.

The mercenary world has also come full circle. In the 1960s the Congo was saved from tribal terror by white mercenaries who were later suppressed (with UN help) by the ruthless dictator Mobutu. The Congo mercenaries had a bad press, and the image of mercenaries in Africa sank to an all-time low thanks to the murderous incompetence of ex-Para NCO Costas Georgiou (alias 'Colonel Callan') in Angola during 1976. However, twenty years on Executive Outcomes, a South Africa-based security company, brought peace to Sierra Leone

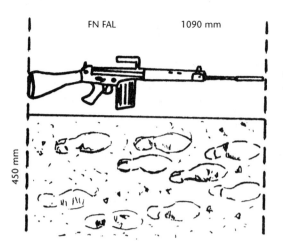

Tracks
To get a rough estimate of how many people have passed down a track, mark out a rectangle as long as your rifle and 450mm (18in) across. Count the number of complete footprints in the box and that's how many people you are following. In practice it is worth adding a safety margin of 2 if there are 5 or more complete footprints, but it generally works for 14 people.

after the UN had refused to get involved in what it feared would be another Somalia-type débâcle. Former South African soldiers (many of them black) with Ukrainian mercenary helicopter pilots defeated a guerrilla movement that had seemed set to take over the government. The methods they used were developed during the bitter years of the Rhodesian War and by the South African Defence Force in Angola and Namibia.

The sheer size of the area of operations will often force you to move more quickly than you might like. During the Rhodesian War, the security forces usually patrolled relatively quickly, walking upright unless in really thick bush which forces you to crouch if you want to see anything. If they had moved in a really sound tactical manner, 'hard targeting' British Army style, they would never have contacted anything. The trick was to locate the guerrillas and bring on a firefight which the security forces would win thanks to superior marksmanship and training.

We used to spend three quarters of our time in Africa on patrol, looking for footprints. You learned to judge the enemy by footprints; you could tell whether they were from FRELIMO or whoever. One technique we picked up was the use of bicycles: you could pedal pretty swiftly and no one questions a bike track. It's also practically silent.

I was sitting on an OP one night in Africa. I had an RPD light machine gun at the ready and was keeping a good look-out. Suddenly I heard a soft 'whoosh' sound and that was it – this guy on a bike just went straight past me before I could react. We never heard him coming. I came back and spoke to Captain Schullenberg about this. I said why can't we use bikes too? We'd just never thought of it.

It is all a matter of tailoring your tactics to the enemy and the environment. The South Africans adopted an even more fast-moving technique in Namibia, where distances are so vast and the population so thinly scattered that conventional infantry patrolling would have demanded untold thousands of soldiers. The Koevoet (South West African Police Counter

Insurgency Division) hunted down guerrilla groups with platoon-sized units of Ovambo trackers. Operating from their big Casspir APCs, which have high chassis and shaped hulls to survive mine blasts, they could move fast through the bush to follow up a contact. Once in close proximity to the enemy, the Ovambo trackers picked up the spoor and literally ran down the enemy, jogging alongside the big vehicles to overrun the guerrillas.

If you are moving along bush roads in vehicles, whether escorting a convoy of civilian vehicles or on operations, remember the anti-ambush drills discussed above. Every vehicle commander should be navigating, not just driving along behind the one in front; if you do get a contact, then everyone knows where you are. Similarly, do not concentrate all the commanders in the same vehicle and make sure your drills for ambush, air attack, mines etc. are rehearsed realistically before you have to do them for real. You might not have South African-style armoured vehicles with their widely spaced wheels and blast-deflecting hulls, but you can improvise some protection against land mines. Add a layer of sandbags on the floor of heavy vehicles and stick to metalled roads if there are any. All vehicles must carry spares and, if possible, try to standardise on the same vehicles so you don't need so many different sets of spares. This also allows you to cannibalise damaged vehicles. If you have to operate off-road, make sure you have some men dismounted if you enter thick bush.

In the South African Army we used to do a thing called 'winter sports': beat hell out of SWAPO just prior to the rains. The winter rains worked to the guerrillas' advantage because they brought low cloud, so our aircraft couldn't operate; the vegetation thickened, and the guerrillas had tons of water. So our aim every year was to go in and beat them before their infiltration started. During the dry season we used to drive them right back, but as soon as the rains started they'd begin moving south again.

Contact in the bush is as sudden as in the jungle. What you do in the first second or two can be the difference between life and death. Again, there is no substitute for rehearsing your contact drills with live ammunition. Dry run-throughs across the volleyball pitch are simply not good enough. Experience has shown that a small force, even when heavily outnumbered, can defeat African guerrillas if it assaults with maximum aggression. Your fieldcraft and fitness must be as good as the enemy's if you are to win in the bush. Do not underestimate the enemy either. Just because the last group you fought were nothing more than an armed mob does not mean the next lot will be the same.

SWAPO were fairly gutsy, but on the other hand in Rhodesia the Shona, which formed ZANLA, were not too keen on fighting. Their ZIPRA allies, mainly formed from the Matabele, were different – quite ready to stand and fight the soldiers. From their point of view, this was not good tactics. We hit one of their camps once and ran into seventy-eight of them. They were going, 'Come on you white bastards!' We were Rhodesian SAS, and like good special forces soldiers we said, 'Whoa, these guys are going to fight, get the fucking gunships!' It's called 'use of assets'!

SWAPO had good clearance patrols, they were very inquisitive and their patrols were aggressive. On the other hand, they were supported by the MPLA (Angolan government forces) in southern Angola, and by other Soviet-sponsored 'visitors'. These were mainly Cuban but we once bypassed a whole load of East German paras escorting a SWAPO unit to the Namibian border. Anytime I came up against SWAPO I had the upper hand; we had gunships and aircraft on call. One thing I can't take away from them is their fighting capability. They would have a go, but they weren't as good as us, and it's no use saying they were. The only reason we used the 'assets', as we called them, was to stop our guys getting killed. Even if we hadn't had air support, we would have still taken their positions.

South African Pathfinders used to operate in twenty-man groups deep inside hostile territory. One patrol ran into a major SWAPO force and, instead of pulling out, tried to hold its ground. What they should have done is upped sticks and got away – 'he who fights and runs away, lives to fight another day' – but they stood and ended up taking casualties as a result. What you have to remember is that when you are in enemy territory you are the terrorist/guerrilla, and you do not stand and fight unless you have aircraft and gunships standing by to support you.

The South African was an awfully gutsy soldier. The young paras I saw in South Africa were as good and as fit as any I've seen in the world, although in some cases they could have done with better leadership. On the other hand, when it came to major operations, big outflanking moves, getting men and material into place, they could do it better than the British Army.

As in the desert, water sources can play a key role in bush warfare. Patrols from both sides may try to use the same water source and they become favourite sites for ambushes. Never walk along well-used game trails for the same reason; the guerrillas might well mine it as you approach. As you patrol forward, concentrate on looking *through* the bush, not *at* it. When your patrol wants to stop, move away from your track just as you would in jungle warfare. Step carefully on rocks or exposed tree roots rather than the earth, so that you leave no tracks. If the enemy is following your trail, he will hopefully carry on in the same direction when your tracks suddenly stop, bypassing your patrol harbour as he tries to pick up the trail again. One useful anti-tracking technique I picked up in Rhodesia was to make an overshoe out of carpet; looking like a large moccasin or snow shoe, it prevented the tread of our boots leaving the telltale imprint in the dirt. You can use sandbags too. We put them on whenever crossing a trail, so we left no obvious marks that would attract the attention of an enemy tracker.

When we went into Mozambique with the Rhodesian SAS, we blacked up totally and wore the enemy's uniforms. We could get away with somebody seeing us at a distance, but not close up. There's no way a white man can walk like a black man. Some guys tried to disguise their tracks by going barefoot like a lot of the locals, but they wouldn't have a piece of skin left on their feet when they'd finished. In any case, even if their feet were sufficiently hardened, they left different footprints. The locals grew up without wearing shoes, so their toes are more widely spread and their prints quite distinctive. Once we had enough, we wore the same boots as the enemy.

The Rhodesians developed a system called 'Fire force' which enabled their very small army to respond to guerrilla activities across hundreds of miles of bush. It used the same principles developed by the Americans a decade earlier in Vietnam, but was conducted on a shoestring compared to the lavish resources of the US Army. However, the success of their relatively tiny force of helicopters and light aircraft is perhaps a more useful model for today's soldier preparing to fight in the bush. Unless you are taking part in a US-sponsored operation, you are probably going to have to make do with whatever aircraft and pilots are available. You are more likely to have a couple of ageing Mil Mi8s than a regiment of American attack helicopters.

Although it was conducted on a very limited budget, every time Fire force came to grips with the enemy it won. If we took casualties, we brought more guys in. But we never lost the impetus of an operation. The reason it was so effective is that it was based on a series of OPs in bandit country, OPs that were in for a very long time. The Fire force was back at base and took off when an OP reported a sighting. The Dakota would be filled up and the helicopters airborne. The helicopters would drop off stop groups and the K car helicopter would be overhead with the commander in it. He'd say, 'Give me six men along such-and-such a line t such-and-such an angle.' The Dakota would come in a drop and sweep line there. Then they would close in.

Sometimes they would pick us up again and manoeuvre sections by helicopter to keep contact. We often used to try to drop right on to the enemy. When the helicopter came down, with the down-thrust of the wind and all the leaves, it scared the shit out of the gooks. We would go straight down and the guys would deploy and start firing. Psychologically it stuffed them. The helicopters came in so low, kicking up a storm of dust through which the enemy couldn't shoot.

You won't defeat the enemy just whizzing above the bush in a helicopter; obviously you need prior intelligence to get the best result out of your slender resources. In the likely scenario that you are involved in a bush war supporting a government against rebel guerrillas, the local security forces will have to be trained and given the confidence to stand up for themselves. But whenever a major contact is achieved, it will probably be up to you to get to the area fast and defeat the enemy. Whatever aircraft you have, get to know them. Practise your helicopter drills until you can do them in the dark, dog-tired and under fire, because the odds are you will have to when you get in the field. Remember that different helicopters have different danger areas.

Pilots will appreciate it if you do not point your rifle at them when getting on the helicopter. In fact, they won't let you on the aircraft if you do, so make sure you can do the drills without muzzle-sweeping anyone. Likewise, do not cock a weapon inside the helicopter. Chamber your first round

HELICOPTER DRILLS
Hand signals

Forget the movies in which they all talk inside the helicopter: in reality it is so noisy as to preclude much conversation, and terrible mistakes can occur when you try to shout instructions above the noise of the engines. These are the basic hand signals used to communicate instead.

A/ Emplaning signal: A thumbs up from the pilot or designated crew member indicates that it is now safe to approach the helicopter. At night you can flash the navigation lights to indicate emplaning, or agree some other signal.

B/ Prepare to deplane: the pilot or crew member indicates thus with his or her left hand. When it is time to deplane, the pilot nods his head vigorously and you must get out in the pre-arranged order as fast as possible.

C/ The right hand raised, palm upwards tells you not to emplane.

D/ OK for some (indicated number of fingers) members of the stick to emplane

E/ Target indication

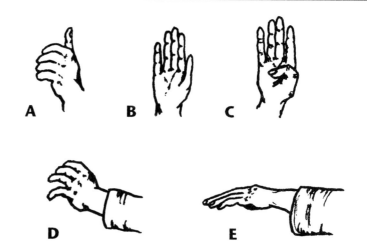

when you hit the landing zone. If you are flying into action, as many of the soldiers as possible should be able to see out of the window. Watch where you are going in case something unexpected occurs. You might come under ground fire or you might spot the enemy on the move.

A lot of navigation in the RLI (Rhodesian Light Infantry) was fairly bad because we did everything from helicopters. The first thing we did in a contact was to fire off a smoke bomb and do everything in relation to that. The whole operation was conducted in a rain of mini-flares. If the guys on the ground met heavy resistance, they'd mark the left and right of their own line with smoke bombs, so the CO in the K car could see the FLOT (Forward Line of Own Troops). Then they'd mark the target and call in the air strike, which arrived from the side. They could put in an air strike fifty metres in front of your position, though we did have men injured sometimes by empty cartridges. One got a broken shoulder, and there was even a guy killed by a 20mm case from a Hunter that landed on his head.

Aerial recognition is critical. Your aircraft must be able to distinguish friend from foe. You can either mark the tops of helmets or sew bright patches of cloth (uorescent material is best) on the inside of a cap. Put the cap on inside out so the helicopters can see who is who during a contact.

We didn't wear helmets in the Rhodesian Army, but we started to use them in the South African paras once SWAPO began to make regular use of mortars. Helmet wearing became part of our SOPs (Standard Operating Procedures) and I used to carry a knobkerrie –

one of those Zulu clubs. If I saw a soldier without his helmet, I'd say, 'Come here!' and (you could do this in the South African Army) I'd whack him on the head, asking 'Did that hurt? If you'd had your helmet on it wouldn't have.' That used to get the message home.

HELICOPTER OPERATIONS

Different helicopters have different minimum areas in which to land, but a typical medium transport helicopter like the widely used Puma needs a circular area with a diameter of at least thirty-seven metres. Imagine another, smaller, circle inside at least eleven metres across. This central area must be sufficiently hard ground to take the weight of the aircraft. You can check this by parking a four-ton truck there; if it does not bog in, the helicopter will be OK too.

Emplaning
You enter the Puma in the reverse order you plan to leave. Take off your hat before you approach the helicopter. Your rifle should be unloaded with safety applied. Your bayonet must be in its scabbard, not on the rifle.

Deplaning
Deplane as quick as you can, lobbing bergens out of the door and get into an all-round defensive position. The first guys out are the members of the two machine gun teams, and they deploy at opposite corners of what will become a roughly rectangular position. The machine guns provide cover for the rest of the stick. The stick leader and his second-in-command end up either side of the cockpit.

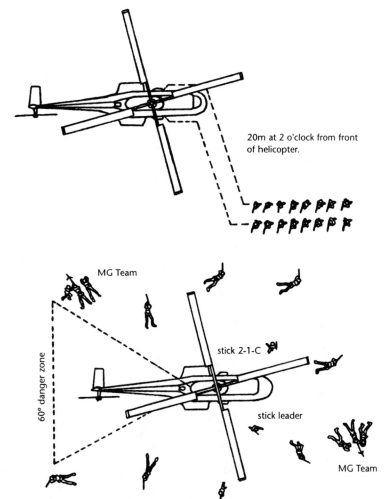

20m at 2 o'clock from front of helicopter.

MG Team

60° danger zone

stick 2-1-C

stick leader

MG Team

Night Landing

The Puma is a typical transport helicopter requiring a minimum landing zone 50 metres in diameter. The central 35 metres of this circle must be clear to ground level and it needs an inner zone (not illustrated here) of 15 metres of hard surface to take its weight (up to 9 tonnes). To guide a helicopter into your landing zone at night, use five torches or other light sources, laid out in a `T' pattern which indicates not just where the LZ is, but what the wind direction is. Torches will need to be partly buried in the ground, at an angle of about 30 degrees. Remember that the down draught from a helicopter is very powerful and you don't want it to scatter your torches or lights all over the shop when it comes in to land.

Emergency Landing

If you have no usable light sources to mark the LZ, you can use two vehicles parked about 25 metres apart. Park them facing into the wind, then turn them slightly towards each other so that their lights intersect at 45 degrees. Make sure all radio aerials are lowered as the helicopter will be passing them at low altitude.

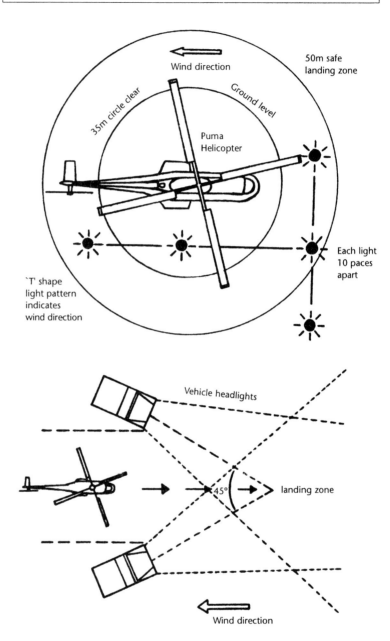

If you are landing several helicopters together, and landing points must be at least thirty-five metres apart (centre to centre) for safety. The landing point should be flat, sloping no more than 124 mils/7 degrees. You can get away with 445 mils/25 degrees if the helicopter just hovers close to the ground while you de-bus.

To board the helicopter, no one approaches closer than thirty metres until signalled to do so by the helicopter pilot or crew chief. Approach from the pilot's two o'clock position so you are clearly in view. Make sure you have folded down any radio aerials before walking under the rotors.

Do not smoke within fifty metres of the helicopter, do not leave bayonets on rifles, and cover entrenching tools with hessian sacking or similar.

Fighting in Arctic conditions

For many years during the Cold War, British forces trained for Arctic warfare in Norway. While a Russian invasion of Scandinavia is thankfully less likely today, you should still be prepared for combat in winter conditions. The Falklands War was a pretty Arctic experience outside Stanley; on South Georgia the SAS faced Antarctic weather conditions stranded on a glacier. The recent UN/NATO deployment to the former Yugoslavia involved prolonged operations in the snow, and there is no knowing where such missions may be ordered in the future.

Winter temperatures are far lower in eastern Europe than in the west. The great Russian offensive that stopped the German assault on Moscow in December 1941 was delivered in daytime temperatures of minus forty degrees centigrade. The Germans found that their machine guns did not function as their gun oil turned to something more like glue. And if you touched the gun with your bare hand, your skin froze to the metal. Optical sights fogged over, blinding tanks and artillery pieces. The German soldiers' boots fitted well, but too well for a Russian winter; their hob-nailed soles conducted the cold very well and there was no room for insulating material. Many a sentry found his toes frozen solid and literally rattling around in his boots and there were tens of thousands of frostbite casualties. Yet in the Russian Army, getting frostbite was a chargeable offence. Russian soldiers were neither as well trained nor as well equipped, but they were used to such awful conditions and knew how to look after themselves. The 'high tech' German Army was beaten.

Countries which experience severe winter conditions might not have the best military equipment in the world, but you might find it carries on working when your kit packs up. A test of NATO rifles in Alaska a few years ago used a thirty-year-old Russian AKM as a control, while all the latest Western designs were put through their paces. Plastic hand guards cracked, magazines fell apart and stoppages were frequent, but the Kalashnikov survived intact. It might not be as accurate on a firing range, but it kept functioning when almost everything else eventually broke.

In Arctic conditions, working parts are much more liable to damage so you must take greater care of your weapons. You will have to wear protection for your hands, so check that you can still get your finger through the trigger guard with mittens on. Keep your mittens dry too; if they are wet, anything you are holding – from a rifle barrel to a hand grenade – will freeze to them. Ice often forms on the working parts after firing and during a pause in shooting ammunition sometimes freezes in the gun. Keep working the bolt or cocking handle every few minutes to prevent such a stoppage occurring.

Machine guns will need a firm base to fire from and are even more likely to get snow in the muzzle or on the working parts, which can be very dangerous. All weapons will require a cover to keep snow from entering the barrel and breech mechanism. Firing on fully automatic sometimes produces a cloud of vapour around the gun. This ice fog can betray your location, so alternative firing positions should be prepared if possible. Soft snow makes it hard to get enough muzzle clearance, so you must put 'feet' on machine gun bipods. You can use ski sticks to keep your elbows from sinking in the snow while firing a rifle.

Mortars require special attention to stop them vanishing, a big steel plate placed on a firing position that you have thoroughly trampled on. If the snow is not compacted properly, the base plate will sink down quickly, causing delays in firing and a dangerous dispersion of the bombs. Soft snow absorbs explosions, making artillery and mortar fire much less effective. However, the ground can be so hard that you cannot dig in without explosive charges, so defending your ground can be more difficult too.

In clear weather, defensive positions are more easily located and vulnerable to air attack, but winter days are very short and hardly get light at all above the Arctic circle. NATO regarded minus twenty-five degrees as the minimum temperature you could expect to fight in; any colder and both sides would have to concentrate on just staying alive. However, in the battle of Moscow mentioned above, the Russian troops were mainly drawn from Siberia where winter temperatures regularly drop below minus fifty. Born and bred in such a hostile climate, they had the confidence in their equipment and knowledge of the conditions to keep fighting when their enemies (however brave) could do nothing but hide in their shelters.

Shelters

If the snow is a metre or more deep, you can dig a snow trench in which to shelter. Shallow snow can be built up into a simple shelter. Insulate with brushwood or whatever is available and remember to dig a deeper hole right by the entrance to your shelter: this will act as a sump for the colder air to sink into.

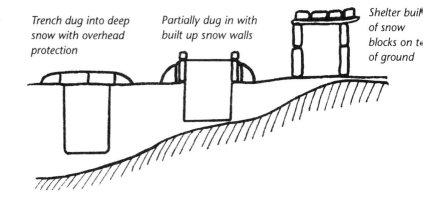

Trench dug into deep snow with overhead protection

Partially dug in with built up snow walls

Shelter built of snow blocks on top of ground

Communications can be a big problem in severe cold because batteries have only a fraction of their normal useful life. If a battery is not being used, it should be on charge. If not on charge, stow it somewhere warm – which usually means inside your smock when you are on the move. Conversely, shouting can work too well. Sounds carry a surprising distance in cold, still air. So noise discipline is very important.

Camouflage and concealment in winter conditions follows the familiar principles of shape, shine, silhouette, smell, sound etc. but a few points should be emphasised. Any heat source – a running engine or a cooking fire – will produce 'fog' as warmed air is cooled quickly to produce condensation. A combination of green/brown camouflage and white overalls is required. Be prepared to adjust your camouflage according to the amount of snow cover. White covers should be worn over helmets and Bergens, and the shape and colour of weapons broken up with white tape.

It is hard to conceal your movement in snow, but you can reduce the ability of the enemy to follow what you are up to if you use the same procedures as we looked at for desert war. Bright sunshine across a snow field can produce very dark shadows across undulating ground, so use shadows or hollows or try to move through trees rather than right in the open. A foot patrol can break up its trail by means of the last man brushing it away. A small vehicle patrol can reduce its trail by following in the tracks of the leading vehicle, with the last vehicle pulling pine branches behind it.

The combination of snow and sunshine makes sharp edges stand out more clearly, making vehicle camouflage harder and any field defences more difficult to conceal. So try to blend in to the lie of the land. If you dig in, you might reach through the snow layer and start throwing up earth – this obviously has to be hidden under now and the bottom of the trench lined with snow as well to avoid it showing up like a thick black line on aerial photographs. As in the desert, the relative difficulty of really concealing your positions from a trained enemy makes the creation of dummy positions especially valuable. You might not be able to hide your presence completely, but you can leave the enemy in doubt as to which positions are actually occupied.

The essentials for winter clothing can be summed up using the mnemonic COLD: Clean clothes; Overheating (avoid at all costs); Loose and layered clothing; Dry clothing. Several layers of thinner clothes will keep you warmer than one thick and heavy uniform; air trapped between the layers is warmed by your body and provides an insulating effect. By wearing several layers of clothes, you can adjust your body temperature more easily too. A big danger is in getting too hot through exertion, like digging in, while wearing full cold weather kit – you work up a sweat which then literally freezes you when you stop work and cool down. The trick is to wear porous layers of clothes underneath a windproof outer layer, for instance jungle lightweight trousers (which dry out fast) under white windproofs. Loose clothes allow more circulation, which is crucial especially for your limbs and feet. During World War Two, German soldiers were initially puzzled as to why the Russians' boots always seemed to be too big for them. As they discovered during the winter, this allowed the Russians to pack their boots with insulating felt but without constricting their feet and reducing circulation to the toes.

MOVEMENT

There is not enough space here to discuss skiing techniques, but in winter warfare skis confer vital mobility that can win battles. Finnish ski troops destroyed road-bound Russian Army units in 1939 by striking behind them, cutting the roads and taking out their supply vehicles before going for the fighting troops. Carrying Bergens and/or towing pulks, military skiing is quite different from civilian skiing, and it takes a couple of winters in Norway to master it properly.

Vehicle movement also demands special skills in Arctic conditions. Simply knowing how to keep engines going is an

Ski signals

Use the following signals to communicate while skiing

A/Patrol will adopt arrowhead formation

B/Patrol will adopt single file

C/Patrol will adopt file formation

D/Patrol will adopt staggered file formation

E/Patrol will adopt extended line formation

F/There is an obstacle ahead

G/Gun or weapons group will move right

H/Gun or weapons group will move left

I/Guns or weapons group to go forward

J/Stop

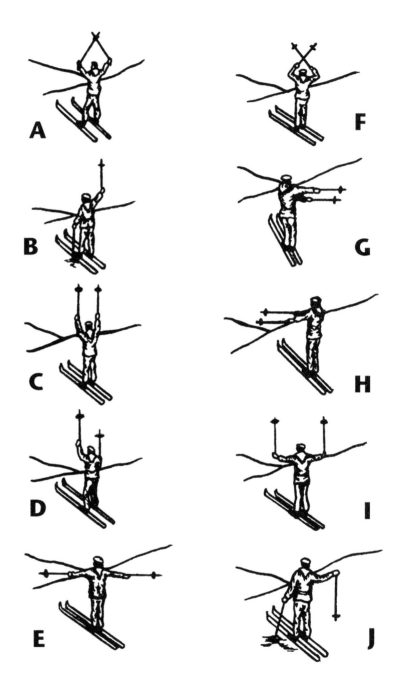

art in inself. Vehicles can also be used to tow groups of skiers in a technique called 'skijoring' in the British Army. Across open snow fields this can allow infantry to move at 10 to 15km/hour, although frequent stops are needed to restore circulation to faces and feet, even when wearing face masks and toe covers. Good route planning is important, since any sort of broken ground will force a halt. Navigation will be discussed later, but it can be especially tricky in winter conditions when heavy snowfalls can obscure landmarks and blur the shape of the ground until it bears little resemblance to the lines on the map. White-out conditions leave you with no horizon to see, so getting any sense of distance is impossible. In extreme cold, wrestling with map and compass while wearing mittens can lead to a severe sense of humour failure. So take enough time to plan your route, avoiding steep slopes or ravines, and try to move parallel to obvious features that can help your navigation – a riverbed, for instance. Alternatively, you can head towards a fixed point like a prominent tree or rocky outcrop. You can use a star at night, but not for longer than twenty to thirty minutes as (obviously) they move in relation to the ground. No sense wandering across a snow field like the Three Wise Men.

Measuring distances can be hard with no features to relate to from the map, and measuring paces with skis on is pretty inaccurate. A better idea is to tie a fifty-metre rope between two skiers; one travels to its fullest extent, while the other stays put. Then they swap roles. Count the number of rope lengths, remembering to measure the actual length of rope between them after they are tied on. This takes a long time, but it is better than nothing when you are trying to be sure.

One blindingly obvious aspect of winter warfare is that rivers and lakes freeze over, enabling soldiers to cross at points normally requiring bridging. In fact, many armies have been defeated because they were not as prepared as the locals to exploit this feature. It takes considerable nerve to drive a tank on to a frozen river, knowing you have little chance of escape if it falls through the ice, so examine the ice very carefully first. Make sure the brain is engaged before putting the body into gear. You will need an auger to measure the thickness of the ice. Do so at regular intervals. Choose a crossing place away from inflow and outflow points of rivers and avoid river bends where the water flow will be faster and the ice thinner.

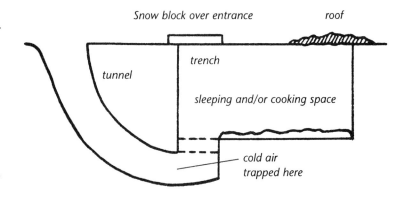

Bunker side view
If the snow is a metre or more deep, you can dig a snow trench in which to shelter. Shallow snow can be built up into a simple shelter. Insulate with brushwood or whatever is available and remember to dig a deeper hole right by the entrance to your shelter: this will act as a sump for the colder air to sink into.

A bunker or 'snow grave' is just a trench dug into deep snow and roofed over, with a tunnel at one end coming back up to the surface. The latter provides ventilation as well as trapping the colder air. The trench should be narrower at the top than at the bottom to make roofing easier. It requires little heat (a single candle) to keep the temperature at around 0 degrees C. even in the Arctic.

Lakes created by hydroelectric power plants, common in Scandinavia, are especially dangerous because the water level under the ice can fall, leaving an air gap of up to twenty metres between the ice and the water surface. There is no escape if you fall through in such conditions. Ice is thinner at the banks, and you might want to thicken it by pumping water on top or by laying down hessian, straw, saplings, or steel mesh to reinforce the crossing point. The first rule of ice safety is not to cross if you are in any doubt about the load-bearing capacity of the ice. Thicknesses of ice required for crossing are:

Load	Ice thickness	Min. distance in metres between load
Man	50mm	2
2-ton truck	200mm	15
2-ton truck	200mm	30
4-ton truck	300mm	30
40-ton truck	650mm	40

COLD WEATHER HEALTH

We will deal with medical problems later on, but this is the logical place to look at the three medical conditions that are an ever-present danger in winter warfare. They can all be overcome by proper training and professionalism. Remember that the Russians made getting frostbite a chargeable offence; the British Army did likewise for trench foot in World War One.

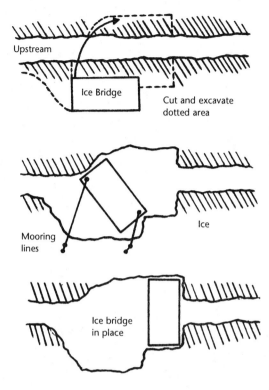

The ice bridge is a tactic dating back hundreds of years: cut a block of ice on a slow-flowing straight section of river and cut away at the area indicated. Secure the ice bridge with mooring lines anchored on pitons driven into the ice, then float it into position to create a crossing. You can secure it better by pumping on water (which will obviously freeze) where it joins either bank.

Frostbite

Wearing inadequate clothing, being exposed to excessive wind-chill or touching metal with your bare hands are all obvious causes of frostbite. The real problem is it can develop without you realising it, especially when you are tired and trying to concentrate on a military task at the time. The numbness arrives gradually, affecting ears, toes, noses etc., so exercise your fingers and toes to keep the circulation going. Work in pairs, with each man keeping an eye on his mate for the telltale waxy whiteness on the skin. At the first sign of frostbite, try rubbing snow on the area until the whiteness disappears and feeling returns. But do so gently; do not rub hard and risk breaking the skin. Many frostbite casualties get into serious trouble because the skin ruptures, leading to an infected wound and often gangrene. This was the grim fate of many soldiers on the Russian front. Warm the area gently, pressing with a warm hand or tucking frostbitten toes under your mate's armpit.

Hypothermia

Like frostbite, this can set in without you realising it. In fact, some survivors remember feeling comfortably warm, and almost drunk. As your body core temperature falls, you stop thinking straight, stumble about and slur your words. Normal body temperature is 36.8 degrees centigrade; hypothermia sets in if it falls below 35 degrees. A warm bath and a hot drink is the cure, but in their absence hypothermia can be dealt with by undressing the casualty and getting him into a sleeping bag with another naked person. Mutual bodily warmth does the rest. If you can lay on a hot bath, do not just dunk the casualty straight in as this can lead to cardiac arrest. Lower them in slowly.

Trench foot

If you stand about for days in wet conditions with the temperature hovering around freezing, the result can be the condition known as 'immersion' or 'trench foot'. The skin looks waxy and swollen, feet feel cold and numb. Nerves and muscles become damaged and the area can become infected, leading to gangrene. It was a major cause of evacuations in the first winter on the Western Front in World War One, and reappeared most recently during the Falklands War. So you must keep your feet dry. Carry spare pairs of socks so you can dry wet ones (under your armpits if necessary) while wearing dry socks. Wash your feet every day, dry them thoroughly and put on dry socks.

Fighting in cities

Cities are continuing to expand, sometimes to the point that they join up to create enormous built-up areas. In western Europe there are nearly 400 cities with populations of over 100,000. Towns and cities in Germany's RhineRuhr area have all become connected; the result today is an urban area of over 15,000 square kilometres containing thirteen million people. Throughout the Cold War, NATO forces trained to defend these gigantic conurbations against the Warsaw Pact armies (who trained and introduced special equipment to capture them). Cities in Africa, South America and, above all, Asia are growing even faster. The sheer size of these places makes it increasingly likely that future wars will turn some of them into battlefields. As demonstrated at Stalingrad, Berlin, Algiers, Hue and, most recently, Sarajevo and Grozny, fighting in built-up areas – or 'FIBUA', as the British Army calls it – is very different from fighting across open countryside. It requires special skills and some special weapons. And unless you have rehearsed your FIBUA drills and know what to do, even the lightest opposition can give you a very bad day out.

The Russian Army's attempt to storm the rebel city of Grozny in 1996 cost it thousands of casualties, and the Russians failed to hold it in the face of determined resistance by the Chechens. Local knowledge is very useful when fighting in a built-up area, and the Chechens exploited this well against Russian soldiers who hadn't a clue about the local geography. It is also very difficult for an attacker to get an accurate idea of how many defenders there are and where their main positions are located. A handful of determined soldiers can hold up far larger forces. Just determining the source of incoming fire is hard enough: there are lots of concealed firing positions, especially if the city has been bombed, and the 'crack' and 'thump' of rifle shots echo off surrounding buildings. Snipers are especially dangerous in an urban battle. As bullets and shells strike buildings, the air rapidly fills with dust and smoke, adding to the confusion. Radio communications usually break down too, since reception by VHF radios is affected by tall buildings. You can put aerials up into the roofs, but if the situation develops fast, you won't have time. Helicopters are useful for co-ordinating your forces and for spotting enemy positions, but they are also vulnerable to ambush by heavy machine guns set up in roof spaces or from shoulder-fired SAMs.

The most obvious feature of fighting in built-up areas is that combat is often at very close range. Fighting with modern weapons inside buildings leads to severe casualties for both attackers and defenders. Just because the SAS have managed to storm buildings, kill half-a-dozen terrorists and rescue their hostages, you should not run away with the idea that this is somehow 'normal' for a 'house-clearing' operation. Without taking anything away from the SAS's achievement at Prince's Gate, the terrorists had made no attempt to prepare the building for defence while the assault teams had rehearsed the attack down to the last detail. If you are fighting your way through a town, you will not have the luxury of minutely planning and rehearsing how to attack every building in every street. You won't know exactly how many enemy are in each location, nor what they are armed with. All you can do is to stick to tried and tested principles – and train hard.

STREET-FIGHTING EQUIPMENT

You will be moving through doorways, windows and holes blown in the side of buildings, so drop your Bergens at a safe point before reaching the start line. You will need to organise your belt order to carry as much ammunition as possible, as ammunition expenditure is enormous during any urban battle. Eye protection is also well worth while. American SWAT teams don't storm buildings in ski goggles because they are planning a little off-piste action after the assault, they have learned just how much dust and debris flies about in a shoot-out inside a building. And you don't want to be rubbing grit out of your eye the moment an enemy soldier appears in the doorway. Elbows and knees need protection too. Ideally you want pads sewn into your uniform and heavyweight trousers rather than jungle lightweights. Camouflage is a problem too. Many a journalist has commented on how conspicuous British soldiers look as they bimble around the streets of Belfast in DPM uniforms designed for warfare in the open countryside. If you are wearing green/brown camouflage, cover it in brick dust and ash to blend in better. And remember: you can never have enough hand grenades!

Special kit required includes the following:

— ladders (aluminium assault ladders ideally)
— ropes
— grapnels
— rope ladders
— torches
— aerosol paint spray
— grenade launchers (essential)
— tracer ammunition (for target indication)
— anti-tank weapon/explosive charges (for blowing entry holes in buildings)
— extra water
— extra dressings and first-aid kit
— prisoner handling equipment

ATTACKING ENEMY-HELD BUILDINGS

A typical domestic house requires at least a squad/section for an attack. When fighting your way into a town, work down both sides of the street, avoiding open spaces by attacking from house to house. Buildings are easier to clear from the top down where gravity is on the side of your grenades. Unfortunately, this is not always possible.

The basic method of storming an enemy-held building is for half the section to provide suppressive fire, while the other half break in and deal with the occupants at close quarters. If you have a covered approach to the building, fine; if not, your suppressive fire must be directed at loopholes, windows or wherever you can see muzzle flashes. Machine gun the roof space thoroughly, since roof tiles offer no cover against full metal jacket ammunition. A 7.62mm machine gun can literally blow holes in a roof through which you might be able to enter the house from an adjoining building. Remember, you can always slap down an assault ladder from a nearby roof and get in that way. Lightly built modern houses offer little resistance to heavy-calibre machine gun fire, and if you have a .50 calibre 12.7mm machine gun, fire long bursts just above where you think the floor level lies. The bullets will penetrate house bricks without trouble.

Assaulting an enemy-held building
(a) The 1st platoon of the Blankshire regiment attacks an enemy-held building: one section delivers suppressive fire against the front of the house, while another attacks under cover of smoke; the third section remains in reserve. Note how you don't try to get in through the doors or windows, but blow a hole in the wall with a mousehole charge.

(b) The first two man assault team blows its way in and the first two men enter, shooting any enemy inside and firing through the walls and ceiling for good measure. As soon as any enemy have been dealt with, shout `Room Clear!' and attack the next room.

(c) On to the next room: the second assault team comes in and attacks the next room, first by lobbing in a grenade, then by charging in and shooting anything that moves. The guys in assault team 1 take up covering positions, watching for enemy counter-attacks which could come through a door or window, or take the form of an anti-tank rocket fired through a hole. The section commander stands where he can communicate with his two assault teams

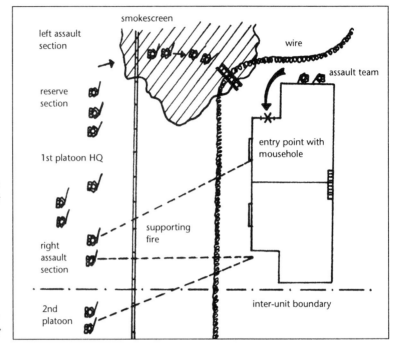

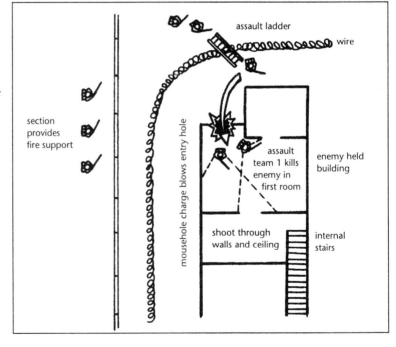

and the link man who can communicate with the rest of the platoon outside the building. Note how you quickly run out of blokes in a modest-sized building.

(d) The assault continues, with the section 2-i-c attacking the next room with one rifleman. The machine gunner joins the section commander and can either support the next assault or fire into the ceiling. This is where the penetrative power of the 7.62mm GPMG is much better than the 5.56mm LSW now in service: it can go through a lot more brickwork! The first two assault teams cover the exterior of the building, ready to shoot down any counter-attacks. Make sure you get ammunition up quickly: you will use a lot taking the building, but need to have enough left to beat off a counter-attack.

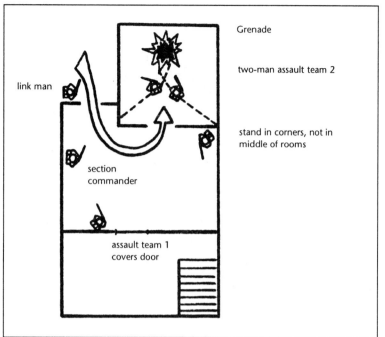

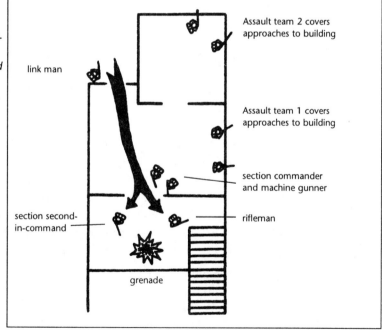

If the enemy has prepared the house for defence, doors and ground-floor windows might well be barricaded or booby-trapped. So make a new door with an anti-tank rocket or an explosive charge (2kg of PE) placed against the wall. Strips of CLC (Charge Linear Cutting) are excellent for this. The ageing Carl Gustav 84mm anti-tank weapon has enjoyed a new lease of life in several armies because it remains a very practical, portable weapon in these situations, even if it lacks the power to knock out the latest generation of tanks. The 66mm LAW, still often encountered, is not really man enough for the job – its HEAT round just does not have enough explosive to make a big hole in the wall. (Not that it would be much fun standing on the other side of it, though.) Remember that you don't have to storm an enemy-held building just because it's there. There is nothing wrong with taking it out with an RPG7, or whatever. Why waste time fighting through when you can neutralise them with your CharlieG or LAW80? With modern grenade launchers you can lob grenades straight into the rooms. Even if it doesn't kill the enemy, it will keep his head down long enough for your assault team to get in.

The best way to make an entry hole is to get a tank to fire its main armament into the building. Tanks are very vulnerable to infantry anti-tank weapons in a town, where every alleyway can conceal a man with a rocket launcher, but if you can support them with infantry, they are extremely effective.

As you approach the enemy-held building, do so by back gardens, rooftops, or the sewer system (usually booby-trapped by an alert enemy, but worth checking). At all costs avoid moving in the street where you can be picked off easily. Plan every move beforehand; one false step and your whole section could be mown down by a concealed automatic weapon, or someone could get picked off by a sniper. If you reach a corner, do not poke your head around at head height where the enemy will be expecting it; lie down and take a peek from the deck. If you have to cross a wall, roll over it, keeping as low as possible to present the smallest possible target.

Built-up areas, as I have said, are a sniper's paradise: stacks of firing positions and escape routes in an environment that is already so noisy that locating his or her position is very difficult. I say 'his or her' advisedly as women snipers have come to prominence in a number of battles in big cities from Stalingrad to Hue city, Vietnam. It was a Russian woman sniper who shot and killed one of the top German sniper instructors during the battle for Stalingrad in 1942. One obvious point here is that you can 'set a thief to catch a thief' and use your own sniper teams to hunt down those of the enemy. Otherwise, make sure you use plenty of smoke grenades to cover your movement. Have machine gunners covering every movement, ready to lay down automatic fire on suspected sniper positions if one does take a shot. Mortaring the rooftops is a good way to discourage them too.

For ease of communication, you can use a colour/numeric code for your location inside the house. The front is 'white', the back 'black', the left of the building is 'red', the right 'green'. Number off the rooms so the second room on the front of the house is 'white 2'.

If you enter a house through a newly blown hole in the wall, dashing in just after the explosion, there is no point wasting a grenade on it. Otherwise, you should always precede your arrival in an enemy-held building by posting a grenade into the room. For added power, you can prepare bunker bombs by replacing the charge in an ordinary grenade with PE. But this can be too effective: one Rhodesian officer got up to the window of an enemy-held building, stood next to the wall like you see in the movies, and lobbed a bunker bomb through the window. The whole house came down on top of him and he was killed.

Now your first two men crash inside, kill any enemy they find and fire into anything that might conceal the enemy, like a doorway or big bits of furniture. This is where training pays off – it takes a great deal of mutual confidence to bust into a room full of enemy and shoot your way methodically through them. The principles are the same as the fire and manoeuvre by pairs we looked at earlier; the difference is that this is fast, furious and at such close quarters that you have little time to recover from a mistake. As soon as you are inside, get away from the entrance. This applies whether you have just blown your way in or broken in through a door or window. If there is someone inside still capable of fighting, they will be covering the entrance. Experience shows that it's the third man through who usually gets shot if the occupants are still firing. One or two men can get inside before the enemy has time to react.

As soon as the room is clear of active enemy, shout 'Clear!'

and cover the door to the next room. In come the next two members of the section and the assault continues, leapfrog fashion, until the house is cleared completely. Before you move on from a room you have taken, fire into all the walls and the ceiling too. Modern floorboards will not stop a 7.62mm round, and even 5.56mm will penetrate some of the time. If the enemy has failed to sandbag the upper floors you might be able to shoot them before you even see them.

I did a house in Botswana with the Rhodesian SAS. We knew terrorists were in the house, so we moved up and assaulted it from the front and both sides. (We couldn't get at the back because of a wall halfway down the garden.) I led the team up and blew a whistle. Each guy threw a bunker bomb through a window. The explosions were so deafening that when I went in, I never realised that a guy was shooting at me. I couldn't hear a thing. Most of the house had come down, but there was a bit still standing and this guy firing away. The High Command wanted an example made of this house, so we left 30lb of explosive in there on a thirty-second fuse. We went back up the road, and half a minute later, whoomf. There were roof tiles fluttering down all over the place.

At the School of Infantry they teach you to show the building has been taken by draping enemy bodies out of the windows. On exercise this can be a bit of a laugh, but it illustrates the important point that it is very easy to end up firing on your own side by mistake when fighting in built-up areas. Equally bad, you can have two groups of soldiers each thinking the other was covering a particular building; at the vital moment when the enemy opens fire, no one is looking the right way. So if you have dead bodies spare, put them to use, or use some other prearranged signal or sign that the building has been taken.

Defending a built-up area is a specialist subject in itself, and one which those of a devious frame of mind will excel in. We will look at defence in a moment, but let's return to our attack on an enemy-held building. Suppose you have blown a hole in the side of the building, stormed inside and shot the defenders. You will probably have taken casualties yourself, and you will have used up many of your grenades and a lot of your ammunition. Your team is scattered about the building, absolutely knackered, while you, the section commander, struggle with the radio that worked up to the moment you got inside. Everyone is practically deaf. Unless you have fired automatic weapons inside a building you will not appreciate just how much extra noise and blast you seem to get. This is the point at which an enterprising enemy will put in a counter-attack. Before you know it, roles have reversed. Grenades drop over window sills, long bursts of fire rake every opening but one and then the bad guys are inside. If you are lucky, you find yourself outside, having to do the attack all over again. If you are unlucky, you probably won't have to worry about FIBUA tactics ever again.

So it is vitally important to reorganise as quickly and efficiently as possible after you have taken an enemy-held building. Put your machine guns in place to cover the most likely approaches an enemy counter-attack would come from. Everyone reports his ammo status and any casualties; this information must be relayed back to the platoon commander, even if it means using a runner not a radio. While you wait for more ammunition to be brought forward, you may have to redistribute what you have. Check any enemy prisoners are disarmed and use them to help evacuate casualties. While you reorganise, check the house for booby-traps. The enemy may have bugged out deliberately, leaving something nasty ticking away in the cupboard under the stairs, or just the traditional grenade trap on an interior door frame.

Room-clearing checklist

When entering an enemy-held buiding, you must get inside before they can recover from the grenade you have just posted through the window. Delay will be fatal.

1. Get inside fast, away from the entry point.

2. Entry team pairs fight back to back, to avoid shooting each other.

3. Check what the floor and ceiling are made of – if wooden, you can fire through both to engage enemy below and above.

4. Fire straight through walls to adjacent rooms, but as you get further into the building you will need to co-ordinate this so you do not spray the room you have just captured and shoot your own supports.

5. Mark entry points with the aerosol paint spray – this indicates a known safe route. Remember the enemy might have booby-traps set at windows and doors.

6. Do not go through a door blind – when in doubt, shoot through it first. And remember to check which way it opens before standing in front of it.

ORTONA

The Italian town of Ortona was captured by Canadian troops during World War Two. It was defended by German paratroops with tank support, who had prepared the place for defence and used almost every trick in the book. So although it happened in 1944, the battle is still used today as a classic example of fighting in built-up areas. Some of the key points are:

— Some buildings were blown up by the Germans to block selected streets, channelling the attackers' movement into 'killing grounds' and providing covered ways for the defenders to move along.

— The rubble from these destroyed buildings was often booby-trapped with anti-tank mines, frustrating Allied attempts to clear them.

— German snipers shot the drivers of bulldozers, preventing rubble clearance until right at the end of the battle.

— Defenders tended to hold the ground floor in strength, with a few machine gunners and grenade men on the upper storeys. Rooftop positions were unusual because the Allied artillery kept shelling them.

— Unoccupied or lightly defended buildings were often booby-trapped. In some cases very large explosive devices were placed and detonated once the Canadians had occupied the building. In one case an entire platoon was killed when the house it had taken exploded shortly afterwards.

— The defenders repeatedly infiltrated back into areas thought to have been cleared. Unless a garrison was left in a captured building, the Germans would sneak back and it would have to be attacked again.

THEATRES OF WAR

Roadblocks
Use roadblocks to channel the enemy advance into prepared killing grounds. All obstacles should of course be covered by fire, otherwise the enemy can simply bring up engineers and take your barricades apart. If you have time and resources, all roadblocks like this can be booby-trapped, anti-personnel mines added to them or anti-tank mines buried just in front of them.

DEFENDING BUILDINGS

The German paras in Ortona had no restrictions on what they could do to defend the town. They had stacks of explosive, plenty of time and no lack of experience. You might not be so lucky, but here are some general outlines for defending your positions in a town or city.

The first task is to block off some of the routes into the town so that you do not have to cover as many, and to channel the enemy attack into areas where your weapons can do the most damage. You can demolish houses with explosives or block roads with vehicles, but remember that any roadblock must be strong enough to withstand a main battle tank, and must be covered by fire. Unless there is someone there to shoot at the enemy, an obstacle is merely an engineering problem the enemy can solve in a few minutes. Stopping a tank is not easy, as any firepower demo will show. 'Say goodbye to your parking problems' says the voice-over as a tank hits a Ford Fiesta and squashes it flat. If you do not want to blow a house over the road, try digging an anti-tank ditch and adding a few mines for good measure. Alternatively, a couple of buses on their sides, filled with rubble and angled towards the enemy, can stop most AFVs. If you have the time and the equipment, a road can also be blocked by a square or triangle shape made from three or four cars pushed on to their sides. The interior is filled with rubble or cement. Make sure the roadblock is covered, from somewhere to the side, by anti-tank weapons.

You can never have too many grenades in attack or defence, but in defence you will never have enough razor wire either.

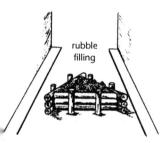

telegraph poles, lamposts etc.

The log crib should use logs, telegraph poles etc. at least 8in (200mm) thick with plenty of rubble inside. Add anti-personnel mines to the barricade and anti-tank mines in front of and just behind it.

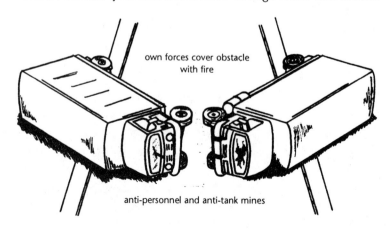

own forces cover obstacle with fire

anti-personnel and anti-tank mines

Enemy approaching from here

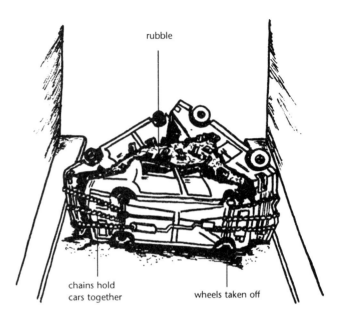

Again, make sure every obstacle is covered by fire or they will get a vehicle up to squash the wire down or just get out the wire cutters and get on with it. Use wire to block up paths you do not want to use, to create obstacles inside houses – choking the stairs with it is a nasty trick – or back gardens. The odd grenade trap among the wire obstacles will deter enthusiastic attempts to clear them quickly. Make sure wire is securely anchored to the floor and ceiling if you fill a room with it; that way the enemy cannot push his way forward using a door or something as an improvised shield. Wire is also useful for blocking off the roof from enemy attack from adjacent buildings, or even to prevent landing on the building from a helicopter.

You will seldom have enough time to prepare buildings for defence – there are so many things you can do to make an attacker's life a misery. So your first priority is to make sure you can cover your arcs of fire from the building, and loophole the walls accordingly. While some of your men get to work on this, you should make a quick list of defensive measures and decide the order in which you will tackle them. If the enemy does allow the luxury of time, then you might be able to complete the lot, but you will usually find yourself in action before then.

If they are still operating, switch off the gas and electricity. Gas is an obvious hazard and electricity is unnecessary – if the enemy does attack at night, you will know the layout of the building and he won't. So fight in darkness to give yourself another edge. By the time you have barricaded the place properly, the building will be pretty gloomy even by daylight. The lack of light and the wire obstacles you place in windows and doors will buy you valuable time if the enemy manages to get inside. Once the enemy is inside a room, evacuate it, let them all in, then post grenades through interior loopholes or doorways. Remove the drainpipes from the house – the enemy can climb up them – and use them around the building (inside and out) as 'grenade chutes'. Remember that lobbing grenades around in a building can be as dangerous for the men throwing them as for the enemy. All too often the grenade hits the doorpost or ricochets off the window ledge. Having a thunder flash fall back at your feet might be a laugh on exercise, but you really don't want to see a live fragmentation grenade rolling back down the corridor.

You can make it harder for enemy entry teams by mining and wiring the approaches to the building. A couple of rolls of wire well secured to pickets with anti-personnel mines sown under the wire will hamper any attempt to rush the building. If you have claymores, then position at least one to sweep each wall. Trip-wire detonation is probably the best option, but a command-detonated mine let off just as the enemy lays his charges against the wall will obviously have maximum effect. The downside is that enemy fire might cut the wire to your mine(s).

Change the layout of the building to further disorientate the enemy troops that manage to break in. Block up the stairs with masses of barbed wire and cut holes in the floors of upper-storey rooms; use a ladder to get up and down. You can always pull it up if you have to evacuate the lower storey. A double layer of sandbags placed on the upper-storey floors is essential if you plan to occupy them. Otherwise, once the enemy gets a foothold on the ground floor he can fire machine guns straight through the ceiling and kill you from there. The same applies to doorways: block them up and knock mouse holes through the walls instead. The attackers will be confused and will waste time trying to get to grips with the maze you have created. It gains you time to evacuate threatened rooms, slip out of the place altogether, or counter-attack.

How to turn a house into a fortress

It takes a lot of man-hours to turn a house into a strongpoint like this, but don't be put off by the size of the task. Prioritise and get on with it, so you can get as much done as possible before the enemy attack. A thoroughly fortified building can hold out against far superior enemy forces: at Stalingrad in World War Two a Russian NCO and his men held off the Germans for weeks using techniques like these.

1. Observation holes knocked in the walls.

2. Observers sit well back so they are not visible.

3. Chimney should be blocked to stop enemy on the roof posting grenades or (in case of very big chimney) arriving like an armed Father Christmas!

4. Mesh screens over windows stop grenades. Use curtains or sacking across the windows too, so the enemy cannot see in.

5. Take cover behind a chest-of-drawers full of earth, far enough back from the window that you cannot be seen. Fun options here include removing the floor right in front of the window so if anyone breaks in, they break their neck.

6. Use ladders through holes in the floors/roof instead of the stairs. If you get driven out of the room, you can retreat upstairs, pulling up the ladder with you.

7. Knock mouseholes between rooms and block the corridors with wire at ankle and head height, or obstruct them completely. You will probably be fighting in the dark so the more confusing the layout of the house the better.

8. Mousehole.

9. Drainpipes should be removed to stop the enemy climbing up them. Take them inside and push through the upper floors. Now you have a perfect delivery system for hand grenades in case the enemy breaks in downstairs.

10. and 11. Stairways can be blocked by doors with nails embedded in them.

12. Leave the water on and fill every container you can find with water. You will (a) need to drink and (b) put out fires.

13. Store spare ammo in the cellar.

14. Escape route: a route out, tunneled into an adjacent house or the sewer system is handy. But remember that it is not necessarily one-way. You'll need to guard the entrance in case the enemy attempts to infiltrate that way.

15. Nail shut and barricade all doorways.

16. The house should ideally be surrounded by mines and wire. Side alleys difficult to fire into but useful for an escalading attempt should be blocked with wire too.

1 observation hole
2 observer well back
4 mesh on windows

THEATRES OF WAR

17. Mini-pillboxes inside rooms help protect you from bits of ceiling falling on top of you during enemy artillery attack. Make sure you have got your arcs of fire right before building them.

18. A double layer of sandbags will prevent an enemy inside the ground floor shooting through the ceiling and into you. On the other hand, grenade chutes in the same floor enable you to post grenades into enemy-occupied rooms.

19. Ground floor windows can be blocked up or narrowed or the floor in front of them removed to make it hard for the enemy to get in through them. But remember that a switched-on enemy won't try for the windows or doors, he will attempt to plant explosives against an interior wall and blow a hole. Moral: make sure you can deliver fire across every side of the building.

20. Strip the plaster from the ceiling now so it doesn't descend on your head during the battle. You can use the bits to help pack out the sandbags.

3
Block chimney

The enemy will direct heavy fire at the building, trying to suppress your fire by sheer weight of bullets. Don't take up fire positions at the windows, where the heaviest fire is likely to be received. Take cover behind something very solid – a rubble-filled chest of drawers for instance – and position it a good metre or so inside the room so that only someone firing directly at the window is lined up for a shot. This is why your initial decision on arcs of fire is so crucial. Your arcs of fire should interlock, exposing the attackers to a crossfire when they start the firefight. Knock the glass out of the windows to avoid a shower of glass once the battle starts. Use the broken glass (and nails, and anything else sharp and nasty) to cover the floor in front of the windows which the enemy might try to break in through. Hang some wet sacking over the window or use chicken wire – anything you can still see through that might stop a grenade or satchel charge being thrown inside. For a final touch, saw through the floorboards in front of the upper floor windows so that enemy troops breaking in find themselves playing a combat version of snakes and ladders.

Fighting in forests and woods

Fighting in forests and woodland is not necessarily the same thing as fighting in a jungle. Deciduous trees lose their leaves in winter, exposing the area to aerial observation in a way not possible in jungles. The profusion of tracks, fire breaks and rides enable armoured vehicles to operate more easily, especially in European forests. Wood fighting is essentially an infantry business, but some armies (the Russians especially) are more aggressive than others in their use of tanks in such terrain. A forest track you might think twice about taking a Land Rover down is a perfectly acceptable route for a Russian-trained armoured battalion in a hurry.

Tanks can knock over most trees found in a European wood, but there is a good chance of a vehicle bogging itself in among the roots and debris. Even the heaviest tanks will usually stick to the tracks for this reason. Armoured vehicles are of course at their most vulnerable in woodland where visibility is so restricted, and enemy foot soldiers can get close enough to tackle them with portable anti-tank rockets. As photos from World War One show, artillery can blast even the thickest woodland into matchstick-size splinters if it fires for long enough. But such set-piece battles are unlikely these days. In the short term, woods reduce the value of artillery and mortar fire, making it hard for fire controllers to locate their targets.

If you are defending a wooded area, construct your main defensive position well inside the forest. Deploy patrols to the edge of the wood to observe, but the enemy is bound to direct enough firepower at the easily observed treeline when he begins the assault. The trick is to delay and disrupt the enemy attack by mines, obstacles and ambushes inside the forest, inflicting casualties and keeping the picture confused. By the time the attackers reach your main position in the heart of the forest, they will be disorganised, low on ammunition and with key personnel among the casualties. That's the theory, anyway. Your forward patrols should identify the main thrust of the enemy attack, so you can bring down your own mortar or artillery fire on them.

If the enemy enjoys a big advantage in artillery and/or air

support, then it is in your interest to fight the main battle with your forces as close to the enemy as possible. This worked very well for the Viet Cong in Vietnam and the Russians in World War Two, luring the enemy into the jungle (or in the Russians' case, the big forests of White Russia) where the defenders had prepared interlocking bunkers that were difficult to see when you were standing on top of them. By fighting the battle at point-blank range, you make it impossible for the enemy to call down supporting fire which would probably kill more of the attackers (who are not in bunkers) than the defenders.

Wire and mine forest tracks you do not want to use. As usual, cover any such obstacle with fire or the enemy will find his way through faster than you think possible. Barbed wire works best when concealed among long grass and vegetation, anywhere where it comes as a nasty surprise. As enemy forces advance into the wood, your obstacles should help channel them into pre-planned ambush sites where you have partly cleared the fields of fire. Don't make the mistake of hanging on too long against a major enemy force. Most casualties suffered in an ambush get hit in the first few seconds, so do the damage and bug out before the enemy outflanks you. As your fighting patrols fall back on your main position, use pre-planned mortar or artillery shoots to help them break contact. Remember that your patrols want to arrive back on the main position in plenty of time, not with the enemy right on their heels.

Your main defences should be built along the lines described in Part One under 'Defensive battle'. Note that in wood-fighting the big danger is that the enemy can break through to either flank and get round behind you. You must pay special attention to communications with units on your flanks, and make sure your defences are sited to deal with an attack from the flank or rear.

If you are attacking enemy forces in a forested area, you now know what to avoid. Try to identify the main enemy position without committing everything you have. Work around the flanks of enemy defences, but stay alert to the danger of pushing down the one track that hasn't been blocked with wire and felled trees. The 'easy' route is probably the ambush site. Counter-attack enemy ambushes with maximum aggression, then you might be able to catch the ambush parties as they make a break for it.

If you find yourself up against a small enemy patrol in a

THEATRES OF WAR

wood, you might be able to drive the enemy into the fire of 'stop groups' that have gone forward to cover obvious escape routes. On such 'sweep' operations, pay special attention to the undergrowth directly in front of you, looking through it rather than at it. Work in pairs, one man moving from tree to tree, covered by the other. And remember to look up. Treetop snipers don't last long in major wars because they die in a hail of mortar fragments, but in rearguard actions which don't involve trashing the whole area with HE, they are are very dangerous.

Keep your assault group behind the line of sweeps. When you encounter serious opposition, the sweep line goes to ground and fires back. Use tracer to indicate target positions you manage to locate. Meanwhile, the assault group manoeuvres to deliver an attack from the flank. It is all basic fire and manoeuvre, but with the added difficulties of poor visibility and degraded communications (radios don't like woods either). So yet again it is down to rehearsing the co-ordination of sweeps and assault groups using live ammunition. There is great danger of a 'blue-on-blue' in a wood fight, and the only preventative is thorough practice which builds the confidence and ability to keep a position under accurate fire while your mate gets close enough to post a grenade through the bunker slit. Talking of grenades: do not throw them about unless the field of fire is clear. They are apt to hit a tree trunk and bounce back.

Fighting at night

As the accuracy and range of modern weapons have increased, so more and more battles are being fought at night. Attackers use the cover of darkness to get close enough to deliver an assault before the defenders can shoot them down. The British Army has a long history of successful night attacks, from the Somme (14 July 1916 – not the daylight disaster on 1 July) in World War One to El Alamein in World War Two and all major attacks we made in the Falklands. Goose Green, Tumbledown and Wireless Ridge were all assaulted in the dark. The Argentines were not able to exploit their fields of fire, and in the terror of the night their conscripts lacked the mutual confidence that comes from hard training. Many of their riflemen either fled or took shelter in the bottom of their trenches, leaving the battle to be conducted by their machine gunners and snipers. Ironically, the latter had better night-sights than the British, making them very dangerous indeed.

In Rhodesia we didn't have much night-vision kit because of the sanctions, so we made good use of the moon, by means of moon tables. My squadron commander in the Rhodesians SAS would come in howling like a werewolf when the full moon was on. A lot of people have forgotten how to use the tables. The first thing I do when I go anywhere on a job is to ask for a set of moon tables, and everybody looks at me like I'm an idiot. We'd use the dark period to move up to the edge of an enemy camp, and when the moon rose at, say, two a.m. we'd hit the place. We timed our operation to infiltrate during the dark period before moon rise. The moon is still important even when you do have night-vision aids. Even third-generation night equipment is very tiring to use for any length of time. The early sets were awful. I once led a patrol down to the river Zambezi for a crossing into Zambia, leading the guys while wearing a pair of night goggles. At the end of the night I couldn't see a thing. My eyes were just pure red and I was knackered.

Fighting at night seems incredibly difficult, but with experience and training you can overcome the obvious difficulties, giving you a big advantage over troops who have not prepared for it. An understanding of night vision is useful. Eyes take longer than you think to adjust to changes in light conditions – about thirty minutes are required for them to adapt to any alteration from complete light to darkness or from clear moonlight to overcast moonlight. Once your eyes have adjusted to darkness, your night vision can be lost in an instant if you are exposed to bright light like a flare or gun-flash. The degree to which your night vision is degraded depends on the brightness of the light you encounter, how long you look at it and how close you are. So long as a flare doesn't go off right next to you, and you look away immediately, you will get your night vision back in a few seconds. But if you have to peer at a map by torchlight, or get dazzled by vehicle lights, you might have much longer to wait.

Night vision checklist

1. If you encounter unwanted light, close one eye. Back in the darkness, if one eye has retained night vision, you will see fairly well. If you don't have to keep one eye open during your exposure to the light, then shut both of them.

2. Avoid looking directly at the light source.

3. Put red filters on your torches, lights etc. This has much less effect on your night vision than white light, but remember that you won't be able to see red or yellow markings on a map.

Your eyes work quite differently by night, and it is important to realise their limitations. You cannot see detail as well at night, so you cannot rely on minor details for vehicle recognition and other tasks. Remember that recognition training should cover recognition by night as well as by day. You have to rely on more obvious features such as the general outline of a human target or the basic shape of a vehicle hull or tank turret. All colours are seen as tones of grey, with red ones showing darker than blue. Although it can be much harder to spot a stationary target, your eyes will detect movement pretty well, especially out of the 'corner of your eyes'. Once your eyes have adjusted to the darkness, you will see objects better if you do not look straight at them. To study something more carefully, hold your arm out at full stretch and form a fist, then look a fist's width away from whatever you are trying to examine.

One disturbing feature of night vision is that your eyes get tired very quickly if you stare at something. In fact, staring for too long can seem to make an object vanish. Rest your eyes a little and it will come back. Because it takes your eyes longer to absorb the little light that is available, and targets lack colour and detail, you must observe more carefully than you would by day. You cannot scan your arcs anything like as quickly. Fix your eyes on a point, count to three slowly, then move on to another point about a fist's width away. Carry on rotating until you have covered your arc, then begin again. Simply peering around is not good enough. Give your eyes a break after a few minutes, then carry on.

The amount of light available can vary enormously at night, making a significant difference to how far you can see. The following table gives the approximate distance (in metres) at which you should be able to spot a single, stationary soldier standing up:

	Light conditions/Background		
	sky or snow	grass	ploughed earth
Full moon	300	150	100
Half moon	150	75	50
Starlight	50	30	15

One simple survival mechanism comes into play at night: your hearing becomes more acute as your vision gets poorer. So it's a case of 'stop-listen-look', rather than 'stop–look–listen'. As this is the case, make doubly sure your equipment isn't rattling and banging as you move. I've listened to a whole company jumping up and down, and all you could hear was the creaking of their kit and the sound of their boots; no metallic rattling, no rustling of Gore-tex.

Thorough reconnaissance is an essential pre-condition to any night operation. The British attacks outside Port Stanley worked well because the enemy positions had been recce'd over a period of weeks leading up to the assault. One reason Goose Green began to go wrong was that there were a lot more Argentine troops there than expected. Night operations are confusing enough without nasty surprises like previously unidentified bunkers blocking your way.

Any night operation should be kept as simple as possible.

'Multi-phase' attacks or anything involving widely separated forces converging at set times should be avoided. The more complicated the plan, the more likely it is to go wrong. If everyone knows the axis of advance, where the boundaries will be etc., you will hopefully avoid 'friendly fire' and the battle will unfold as planned. Similarly, do not rely on a fixed time at which to begin the attack. Night approach marches often take a lot longer than you planned, so the final order for the attack should be given over the radio when everyone is in position.

'Silent' attacks are often recommended (particularly by armies without much artillery) on the grounds that you can sneak up on the enemy defences during the night and deliver the attack to take them by surprise. Once the shooting starts, the attackers' artillery joins in, but does not fire off stacks of ammunition in a preliminary bombardment. Of course, this does rather assume that the enemy will not have patrols or OPs covering his front and does not own any modern night-vision devices. As with any battle tactic, you have to tailor your plans to your opposition. If you can catch them in their sleeping bags, then a silent attack might be better than starting off with a bombardment that wakes them up and gets them armed and ready in their trenches. On the other hand, silent attacks were rumbled pretty quickly in the Falklands and might have been better being 'noisy' from the start. Remember that it is not just the enemy who can turn a 'silent' attack noisy: having one of your own men step on a land mine as you get on to the start line is just as likely. Either way, try to avoid the obvious approach route to the enemy position; the enemy will probably have his artillery pre-registered on the spot, enabling the defenders to call down fire instantly.

The Falklands campaign was unusual because neither side deployed main battle tanks to the operational area. Even so, the handful of CVR(T) vehicles taken by the British Task Force did come in useful. In conventional operations, especially attacking defended positions by day or night, tanks and armoured vehicles are going to play a key role. Modern tanks and infantry-fighting vehicles have enough night-vision devices to fight right around the clock. (It was the exhaustion of the crews, not the darkness, that eventually halted Israeli armoured attacks in the Yom Kippur War.) So your night operation might well involve armour. Mixing tanks and foot soldiers in the same place at night usually leads to someone getting run over, so in a mechanised force infantry will tend to assault in their vehicles, dismounting as close to the objective as possible. Supporting tanks can approach the objective on a converging course from a different direction, or accompany the IFVs directly. Tanks can illuminate any target within a kilometre or so with their searchlights, but they will not want to stop for very long, lit up and vulnerable.

Night fighting may also be forced upon you by the enemy's tactics. In Rhodesia and Angola/SW Africa, where the security forces dominated the air, the guerrillas attacked late in the day or in the evening when they would have the longest period in which to escape under cover of darkness. In Rhodesia they tended to attack in late afternoon, and in south-west Africa, if SWAPO planned to hit you, they would always do so before midnight.

The following points sum up the reasons why fighting at night can be a useful tactic to employ:

— The chaos and confusion of a night battle gives well trained soldiers a big advantage over badly trained/poorly motivated opposition.

— Enemy aircraft will have great difficulty supporting their ground troops if you attack at night.

— Counter-attacks are harder to co-ordinate at night, so you will be more likely to hold the position you have captured.

— Enemy mortar and artillery fires will not be as well directed.

— Defensive positions often fail to provide mutual support, enabling the attacker to slip between them and attack from the flank.

LIGHT SOURCES

1. White Light

Searchlights have often been used in night battles, but they are obvious and easy targets for enemy fire. White light is more normally provided by flares, especially parachute flares delivered by artillery or mortar rounds, but every gun or mortar firing illumination rounds is one fewer shelling the enemy with high explosive. White light can be a big aid to navigation and allows more effective fire and manoeuvre against the enemy. It also attracts a lot of attention, which can make it a useful deception measure, keeping the enemy occupied while the real assault force gets into position.

2. Active Infra-Red

Active infra-red systems direct a beam of infra-red light at the target. This is reflected back to a viewing device. Useful for locating key targets like enemy machine gun positions or weapon pits, active systems have the disadvantage that there are infra-red detection devices available, and the user of an active system has no way of knowing if the enemy has detected it. You might not know you've been spotted until it starts raining mortar bombs. Active IR systems were fitted to many Warsaw Pact vehicles and were widely used for night operations, so if your opponent is Russian-trained or equipped, they may do the same.

3. Passive Infra-Red

Passive infra-red systems monitor the amount of infra-red energy given off by such things as tank engines or gun barrels. Also known as 'thermal imaging', such systems are undetectable but less precise. It also takes a lot of practice to recognise the 'thermal signature' of a vehicle, which rarely bears any resemblance to the vehicle's actual appearance and is quite different depending on whether the engine is hot or cold.

4. Image Intensification

Image intensifiers simply magnify the ambient light by a factor of 100,000 plus, and on a moonlit night they are very effective. They can be detected by other image intensifiers pointed the other way, and they are not nearly as effective on a cloudy night. Most image intensifiers are rather fragile for military operations and you will often find it is broken when you need it the most. Flares 'blind' most image intensifiers and their operators if they burst suddenly in your field of view. However, a set of functioning image intensifiers fitted on the rifles of a team of professional soldiers can make for a satisfyingly one-sided night fight.

Ground radar can be useful too, well-trained operators being able to detect targets regardless of the light conditions or weather. However, any radar set is detectable and can either be jammed or just marked on the map and blastedby enemy artillery.

3 COMBAT SURVIVAL

Battlefield first aid

I've mentioned the need to plan for what you'll do if you take casualties. This is particularly critical for a small patrol, where a couple of casualties can effectively occupy the whole patrol as a wounded man requires several men to get him to safety. Obviously there are going to be times when you can't afford to devote all your manpower to bringing in the casualties – leave no one engaging the enemy and you'll be overrun. But in addition to rehearsing your actions on taking casualties, you need to be able to give effective first aid.

In the British Army one man in each section is supposed to be trained as a combat medic. But what if he becomes a casualty himself? Everyone must not only know the following battlefield first-aid techniques, but he must practise them regularly. Like everything else in this book, it is one thing to read about it or listen to the lecture, but quite another if you have to do it for real. So rehearse.

The first rule of first aid is simple: don't get shot yourself. This is where it can be hard to adjust from peacetime training to real combat. War is about dying. The bullets don't stop when someone gets hit. The enemy will be delighted if you forget everything you've learned about fire and manoeuvre in your haste to rescue a casualty. And if you become a casualty yourself, someone else is going to have to risk his life to bring you in. So don't stop thinking tactically the moment someone gets hurt. Bringing back a casualty under fire is incredibly dangerous, which is why it features in so many VC citations and why most of the half-dozen double VCs were medical officers.

If someone's triggered a booby-trap, there could be more about, ready for the unwary feet rushing to the rescue. This is especially true in counter-insurgency operations where the terrorists/guerrillas rely on such tactics rather than stand-up fights with the security forces. If the casualty results from a vehicle crash, make sure you have turned off the engine before doing anything else.

This may sound hard, but you are not always going to stop to give first aid. If you are in the middle of a firefight, getting forward using fire and manoeuvre, you cannot afford to lose momentum by stopping for casualties. If you do, the advance will break down and the enemy will win. You will suffer additional losses as a result. The best way to stop your unit taking further casualties is to stop the enemy firing. Close with the enemy and kill him. Then attend to your wounded.

The same applies in defence. If you all cease fire to look after the wounded, the enemy will steam over the position and you will all be killed or captured. In theory, if you are fighting from four-man battle trenches as per the current pamphlet, one of you can stop to deal with a casualty. Since this halves your firepower, it is only realistic when the enemy is still some way off and plenty of other weapons are in action. If the opposition is nearly within grenade range, you had better deal with them first.

No matter how badly smashed up the casualty is – many injuries look much worse than they are – reassure the man, and tell him what you're doing as you administer first aid. Keep the man's confidence. If you turn pale and can't look him in the eye, what confidence is he going to have? Your job is to keep him going until he can receive proper treatment.

Once your casualty is under cover, check him out completely. Don't just deal with the first injury you see, follow this order of priority: A, B, C, D.

A: AIRWAY

A casualty's airway can be blocked in a number of unpleasant ways. It can be choked with vomit or blood, or blocked with mud, smashed up teeth or other debris. An obstructed airway can be obvious, e.g. head stuck under water, or less apparent, e.g. blockage inside the throat. So check the casualty's breathing. Is it very laboured? Bubbly? Whistling? Is his/her face pale or even with a blue tinge? You have to act quickly since it only takes a few minutes without oxygen to inflict permanent damage on the brain. Death takes little longer.

Clear the airway of any physical obstruction. Check the mouth and throat are clear, scoop out any vomit or whatever is obstructing the airway. Open the casualty's airway by the 'jaw thrust manoeuvre': place the first three fingers of each hand either side of the chin, behind the casualty's lower jaw, and extend the casualty's neck by bringing the jaw forward. Now place the casualty in the recovery (three-quarters prone) position. Kneel on one side of the casualty and tuck his near-side hand under his body and the other over his chest. Cross the far foot over the nearer ankle. Supporting his head with one hand, grab his clothing at the hip and gently roll the casualty on to his front. Bend the upper leg to bring the thigh forward and bring the upper arm forward too; this stops him rolling right over on to his front. The idea here is to place the casualty in such a position that no further harm will come to him. Unconscious casualties can often die by choking on their own vomit.

B: BREATHING

The airway is clear, but the casualty isn't breathing. You need to 'kick start' the casualty's lungs by breathing for him in the technique once known as 'the kiss of life'. Note that the Exhaled Air Resuscitation (EAR) technique, as it is called today, is not something to practice on another person. It is also not something to attempt unless the casualty has indeed stopped breathing. So before you do anything:

1. Check that the casualty is unconscious, not simply asleep.
2. Can you hear, feel or see the chest moving?
3. Can you feel any air being exhaled by the casualty?

f the casualty is unconscious and not breathing, the procedure is as follows:

1. Check for a pulse. If the casualty's heart has stopped too, you will need to perform cardiac compression (see below) as well as EAR.

2. Lie the casualty on his back, clear and open the airway. Loosen tight clothing around the neck.

3. Tilt the casualty's head back and pinch his nose shut.

4. Take a deep breath and breathe hard into the casualty's mouth, hard enough to make the chest rise. Remove your mouth and allow the chest to fall. Repeat every six seconds until the casualty breathes unaided. Move him into recovery position.

If the casualty's mouth is too injured to allow EAR like this, you can try to perform the same procedure by blowing directly up his nose.

Cardiac compression

Like EAR, this cannot be practised on a real person. Never perform cardiac compression on someone whose heart is beating, however faintly.

The only reliable way to see if the heart is beating is to check the carotid pulse at the neck (next to the windpipe, above the Adam's apple on the casualty's right-hand side). A weak pulse can be hard to detect at the wrist. When combined with EAR, the procedure is known as CPR (Cardiopulmonary Resuscitation). It works as follows:

1. Position the casualty as for EAR.

2. Give two breaths as above.

3. Check the pulse at the carotid artery.

4. Find the lower end of the breastbone (sternum).

5. Place the heel of one hand there with the other on top, and press down with the weight of your body. Lift your hand to allow the chest to recoil.

6. Repeat once a second, fifteen times.

7. Inflate the casualty's lungs with the EAR method twice.

8. Repeat (6) and (7) until the casualty recovers. As soon as the heart starts, stop the chest compression but keep the EAR going until the casualty can breathe unaided.

If you have two first aiders, one does the chest compression and the other performs EAR every five rather than fifteen seconds.

C: CIRCULATION

The next most common cause of death from injury is bleeding. Proceed as follows:

1. Place the casualty in a comfortable position, ideally with the injured part elevated above the heart (to reduce blood

flow to the area). Thus you can sit up someone with a head wound or raise an injured arm. But think before you start moving the casualty about; you don't want to make existing injuries worse, e.g. by moving someone who has injured his spine.

2. Place a dressing over the wound and apply pressure with the palm of your hand. Don't try to push protruding bones back into place or pull out foreign matter, e.g. bits of glass or metal. Just get the dressing in place and apply pressure. Resist the temptation to take it off and see how things are getting along – this will break the scab and you will be back to square one. If the bleeding soaks through the first dressing, place another one on top rather than replace the one in position. Place a third on top if that fails to stop the bleeding.

3. You can reduce the blood supply to an area by pressure points.

Brachial pressure point
This is at the base of the arm. By pressing into the armpit with your thumb you can stop the flow of blood down the arm.

Femoral pressure point
This is just inside the groin. By pressing here you can reduce the flow of blood into the leg.

In both cases you must not apply pressure for longer than fifteen minutes. When you do release the pressure, do so gradually. If bleeding starts again, you can apply the pressure point again, but only for fifteen-minute periods.

The issue field dressing is a large gauze pad with a bandage attached. You should carry at least three and keep them in the same place(s) so if you are unconscious, your mates can find them and use your dressing to treat you. If you don't have a proper dressing, any clean material will do. Cotton, being absorbent, is ideal. Handkerchiefs or shirts torn and folded are the usual standbys. They should be as clean as possible, but you don't have time to go to the laundry if they're not. Gunshot wounds are notoriously contaminated anyway, the bullet pushing bits of cloth into the wound, and high-velocity rounds cause a temporary cavity that allows all sorts of nasties inside.

D: DISABILITY

Fractures
There are two types of fracture:

1. Open
There is a break in the skin as well as the bone. Often the bone will protrude through the skin or it may be that a bullet has gone through the skin and shattered the bone below.

2. Closed
The skin is intact, but the bone below is broken. In this case, the area will usually swell and bruise. Sometimes it might appear like a sprain, but you should treat it as broken until the medics confirm otherwise.

You need to keep the fracture as still as possible to prevent the edges of the broken bone causing further damage and pain. To immobilise a limb:

1. Remove any rings, watches or garments that might constrict the limb if it swells up.

2. Splint the fractured limb if possible, and don't try to force it back into a 'natural' position. If the casualty has a fractured leg and you can't splint it because of the tactical situation, tie the injured leg to the other one, and put some padding in between. Grab him under the armpits and drag him in a straight line. Do not roll or move him sideways.

3. Apply splints so that the joints above and below the fracture are immobilised. Put some padding between the splint and injured area. This is particularly important between the arms and chest, in the armpits and where the splint rests against bony parts of the anatomy like the wrist or knee.

4. Bind the splints to the injured limb above and below the fracture, but not so tightly that they interfere with circulation.

Burns

Burns can be very painful, and a relatively minor burn might hurt more than a more immediately life-threatening injury. So remember A, B, C, D when dealing with burns. And something else: don't become a burn victim yourself. If the burns casualty is lying in a pool of water next to a bank of electrical terminals showering sparks everywhere, don't wade in and collect 25,000 volts yourself. Before treating the casualty, assess the situation. You might have to extinguish a fire on or near your casualty. You might need to turn off electrical power, or prod an electric cable out of the way with something that does not conduct electricity, e.g. a dry branch.

Burns are still described in the media as 'rst, second or third degree', but this classification has been replaced. Burns are either superficial (they appear tender, red and swollen) or deep (they appear blistered and swollen, the surrounding skin often very red. In the worst cases they are dull white and can appear charred.) In the latter case, the victim might not feel much pain yet as the nerve endings are destroyed.

To treat burns, follow this procedure:

1. Put out flames and smouldering clothing using water or by smothering the casualty in blankets etc.

2. Cool the burned area by pouring water over it. You can use milk, beer or any other harmless liquid, but never pour butter, oil or any sort of ointment on to the burn. The liquid is supposed to stop the 'cooking effect' that continues to do damage even after the source of the burn has been removed. By putting oil or ointment on top, you are sealing in the burn and prolonging the cooking effect.

3. Cover the burn with a clean (ideally, sterile) dressing. Don't pick out bits of charred uniform stuck to the burn before you do this.

4. Administer morphine if necessary.

5. Immobilise a badly burned limb as per a fracture above.

Burns often produce blisters which you should leave well alone. They dehydrate the casualty, so give him frequent sips of water.

If the burn was caused by phosphorus, cover it with a wet

dressing and keep it wet. Don't try to remove the phosphorus yourself.

Shock

This is an expression widely used in TV and radio news reports by ignorant journalists. You often hear of people being treated for shock after a car crash, but in most cases they are actually talking about a nervous reaction to a traumatic incident, not 'shock' in the medical sense of the word. True shock is the body's reaction to the loss of circulating body fluid, e.g. through blood loss or because of a burn. Shock is a common cause of death after injury. Shock exhibits the following symptoms:

- cold, clammy skin
- pale, anxious expression
- fast but weak pulse
- shallow, rapid breathing
- casualty feels faint, weak, dizzy and may have blurred vision
- casualty may be semi-conscious or even unconscious

To treat shock, follow this procedure:

1. Lay the casualty down and make certain his airway is clear and he is breathing.
2. Examine him for any external bleeding and deal with any that you find.
3. Elevate his legs above his head, provided they are not injured.
4. Support and immobilise any injured limbs.
5. Keep the casualty warm, but not overheated.
6. Moisten his lips if he is thirsty but do not give him anything to drink.
7. If he is unconscious, place him in the recovery position.

Sucking chest wounds

'A sucking chest wound', as the saying goes, 'is nature's way of telling you you've lost the firefight.' A gunshot (or piece of shrapnel) that penetrates the chest wall can cause air to be sucked in through the hole, making breathing increasingly hard as the lung collapses and air comes in and out of the hole instead of up and down the windpipe. Then you die. Look for the following symptoms:

1. You hear a sucking sound when the casualty breathes in.
2. Breathing is difficult and shallow.
3. Blood-stained fluid bubbles around the wound when he breathes out.
4. The casualty coughs up blood.
5. There is blueness around his mouth and lips.

To treat a sucking chest wound, follow this procedure:

1. Check and clear the airway.
2. Cover the hole with an impervious material, e.g. a field dressing that covers more than just the wound. Secure with a broad bandage.
3. Place the casualty in the recovery position if unconscious.

Abdominal wounds

Gut shots were rightly feared in both world wars – they weren't the million-dollar wound that got you home, they got you buried. An abdominal wound is still among the most dangerous you can suffer.

The abdomen is the correct description for the bit of you that runs between the chest and the pelvis, often called the stomach. It's where your stomach is, for sure, but also present are the liver, spleen, bowels, kidneys and bladder. Smash them around, jumble the contents and you have a very nasty wound indeed. There is not much a first aider can actually do here, although he can cause further damage by trying to push bits of internal organ back inside before applying a field dressing. Leave it alone and get a dressing or dressings on to stop the blood loss. The other mistake is to allow the casualty to drink anything. Casualties with abdominal wounds must *not* be allowed anything by mouth.

If you can, position the casualty in the 'W' position, knees drawn up to relax pressure on the abdomen, head and shoulders raised. Alternatively, lie him on his side with his knees drawn up. A casualty with abdominal injuries needs to be evacuated as soon as possible.

Moving casualties

You may have to move casualties who are unable to move under their own steam. Once again, this is something to practise. Get the various methods perfected while everyone is fit and you will waste less time wondering what to do if it happens for real. The fireman's lift is still the first technique illustrated in the manual, but it is very uncomfortable for the casualty. If the casualty is conscious, piggy-back works better, but both these methods make you a large target in a tactical situation. Methods involving two men carrying the wounded, such as 'the seat' (where two of you make a seat with linked hands), obviously make an even bigger target.

If you need to move someone under fire, you can drag them along with their arms folded across their chest like an Egyptian mummy. Another scheme that works – although it's good for a laugh when practising – is the neck drag. Tie the casualty's hands together, lie him on his back, kneel astride and place his wrists behind your neck. Taking his weight on your neck (it's a great way to make new friends) you crawl slowly forward. This is utterly knackering, and the basic dragging along technique is usually preferable. Ideally, drag the guy along with your left hand only, keeping your weapon in your right hand ready for action.

Escape and evasion

You can find yourself cut off behind enemy lines in all manner of ways. Aircrew eject from a crippled fighter, or a soldier finds himself alone but alive after a patrol is ambushed deep into enemy territory ... Either way, it is up to the individual to survive, to evade capture and get home.

As with all the activities described in this book, the time to learn the skills required for successful escape and evasion is not at the moment you suddenly need them. Anything you carry by way of a 'survival kit' should be used regularly so you don't have to learn on the job. And make sure you do carry it on you, not in your Bergen, which you might well lose in whatever disaster leaves you doing E&E for real. Physical strength is a major advantage in this situation, especially the confidence that comes with a high standard of unarmed combat skills. This can make you a hard person to capture in the first place, and give you a useful edge when it comes to an escape attempt.

The basic rule, developed by the SAS, is that you live on the contents of your Bergen while your belt order holds the ammunition and grenades to fight with. You survive on the contents of your pockets. So, your combat jacket pockets should contain a compass, first-aid kit and water-purifying tablets as well as a pocket knife and wire saw. Fire-lighting oil, scalpel blades, condoms (for water carrying, not fraternisation with the locals) and a sewing kit are also useful. For added refinement, place the escape and evasion kit where an enemy soldier seaching you would be most likely to overlook it.

It is an old truth that escape becomes harder the longer you are held prisoner, but if you are captured and manage to slip away quickly, your chances of making it home are much improved if your survival kit is intact. Wire saws can be hidden in the waistband of your trousers, the rings replaced with paracord. Fishing line can be hidden in the seams of your clothing, with fish hooks (wrapped in thick plastic or tape) sewn in nearby. The following list includes all conventional items found in a survival kit. To this I would add snares and lock picks (which are, incidentally, illegal in the UK and some other countries). Anything that increases the risk of an encounter with a potentially hostile civilian is to be avoided, but sometimes a raid on a farm's livestock or burglary of an unoccupied house are the only ways to replenish your supplies.

A good escape and evasion kit would comprise the following items:

- fire-starting kit
- compasses (prismatic and button compass)
- wire saw
- torch
- fishing kit
- pocket knife
- water-purifying equipment
- field dressings
- survival ration
- signalling mirror
- mini-flares
- water bottles
- razor

After a few days without food, you will start to feel weak and a little dizzy. It becomes hard to concentrate and, if the situation continues, your heart rate slows, blackouts follow and you become thirsty, cold and in no condition to keep going. So you must do something about it: hunting, scavenging or stealing. Snares are handy if you are resting up for a night or two, but normally you should aim to do most of your travelling during the hours of darkness. The extremely well-equipped soldier might consider a dedicated survival rifle – an AR7.22 or .22/.410 combination enables you to add the odd bunny or squirrel to the pot, always worthwhile if the extra weight and bulk can be accommodated in your Bergen.

Stealing eggs and/or chickens, it is best to take a little in the hope their absence will not be missed. The mysterious disappearance of a whole bunch of chickens is likely to be reported, especially if the enemy is on the look-out for you. Hill sheep are useful prey because the absence of one will usually go unnoticed. Be careful on lowland farms though. The farmer will probably detect the absence of any animal, but if you butcher it by a stream and bury the bones, you should be long gone before the authorities are alerted. Remember to check the liver of a sheep you kill. If it looks grey and unhealthy or has yellow blotches on it, the animal is diseased and should not be eaten.

If you are going to lie up for a few days, you need to pick a position near water or you will have to take water in with you during the night. The ideal lying-up position (LUP) provides concealment from both the ground and the air and offers a choice of escape routes. Don't enter your LUP until after dark, so it will be unlikely that the enemy observes you in the position. Check the area at first light, looking particularly for tracks (yours or theirs) which might require camouflaging or a change of position. Bury any rubbish and remove any sign of your presence when you move on. And keep your kit handy so that you don't have to leave anything behind if you suddenly have to run for it. If you are part of a group rather than evading alone, then you should have a sentry routine while in the LUP and proceed as outlined in Part One under 'Patrols'.

URBAN AREAS

A lot of escape and evasion training concentrates on how to slip through a rural area without getting caught by enemy troops or security forces. However, you might equally well find yourself on the run in an urban area. Standard advice for evaders is to avoid population centres because any contact with the people involves a risk of compromise. Some parts of the world are so built-up that this is difficult to avoid, so you must be prepared to bluff your way through an urban area. Once again, movement at night is easiest, but it begs the question of where you hide up during the day. It all depends on which part of the world you are operating in.

In many Western cities you could wander through looking like just another vagrant and get away with it, but in others, from Belfast to Beirut, the population is divided on tribal lines. The presence of a stranger would be detected very quickly, usually with disagreeable consequences. Even the 'vagrant strategy' carries risks: in most cities there is an established underworld of 'street people' which might report strangers to the security forces or just stab you for your coat. So keep on the move; any attempt to go static increases the risk of detection. If you look carefully, you can live and survive like a vagrant, trawling through bins outside homes and, above all, restaurants. If you raid domestic homes' bins, you should pick through the contents carefully, remove what you want and stuff the rubbish back in so that it is not obvious that it has been tampered with. Strange as it might seem, experience on SAS escape exercises reveals that a surprising number of people remember roughly what the contents of their dustbin looked like the last time they emptied the bin.

If you are not going to bluff your way through disguised as a tramp, then do everything possible to avoid looking like one. This is why you carry a razor: unshaven men look suspicious, designer stubble only really working with an Armani jacket. Tatty clothes and, most obviously, combat boots are the classic give-aways that betray prisoners of war on the run. If you are on the move during the day, walk with confidence as if you know where you are going. Avoid focal points like railway or bus stations where security forces are likely to be present, and avoid children too. Children and dogs have a good track record of betraying evaders – they pick up on inconsistencies of appearance or smell and are not shy of making it known loudly to everyone in the street.

If you do find a security cordon across the road you are using and you have to cross over, do so at night. The easiest way is to cross just after a car has passed so its lights have destroyed the enemy's night vision. But if you approach a cordon and observe for a while, you will hopefully be able to watch the sentries changing over. Other enemy soldiers will probably betray their location by movement, noise, lighting cigarettes etc. Have patience and watch for an hour or two. Then you can break through because you know their routine and their location.

Bridges should not even be attempted; swim, or use an improvised raft. There is bound to be a guard at one end or the other.

EVASION IN THE JUNGLE

Escape and evasion in jungle (or one of the massive forests of eastern Europe, for that matter) is as much an exercise in survival as anything else. With few well-travelled routes, the enemy will cover all the obvious ones without much difficulty, placing cordons on roads and watching the rivers.

Movement by night will be almost impossible in some jungled or forested areas, but there will be less chance of bumping into someone, so this is not a problem. In most jungles there are really only two types of animal to be afraid of: insects and humans. Most casualties in the jungle are victims of insects (and the diseases they can give you) or humans. We will look at basic survival skills later, but for an evader, one key issue is your relations with the locals; the area may be home to tribes that owe little allegiance to the enemy, or to peoples only too happy to sell your severed head to an enemy patrol.

Thorough recce is essential before you approach a village. If you are trying to establish good relations or there are so many of them that you would be bound to lose a fight, then don't go in waving a gun about. Approach slowly and openly up the main track, so they have warning of your approach and can take a considered reaction, as opposed to shooting first and asking later. Take off your helmet and anything that looks utterly alien to them, because the more you look like them the less likely they are to react in a hostile manner. Treat the old men with respect – they are probably in charge. Extend the most dignified respect to all women in the village, especially if they don't wear bras. Do not make the mistake of thinking they will behave like girls on an 1830 beach holiday just because they're dressed like them. If they help you, do not overstay your welcome as their resources are probably limited and every day you remain there could put them at risk from enemy forces. And however helpful they have been, do not tell them exactly where you are going next. Every village has its Judas.

Prisoners of War

The treatment of prisoners of war is supposed to be governed by the Geneva Convention. I say 'supposed' because not all nation states have signed it, some signatories have tended to ignore it, and guerrillas/terrorists seldom play by the rules either. However, it is important to know 'the rules'; with twenty-four-hour news channels and satellite TV, the media presence in war zones is greater than ever before. Violations of the Geneva Convention are more widely reported and the Yugoslavian wars of the 1990s have stimulated interest in international war crimes trials. So, this famous agreement might save your skin if your captors adhere to it. And if you take prisoners and mistreat them, your chances of ending up in the dock are higher than ever. (On that note, it is worth emphasising that any soldier mistreating prisoners is endangering his own life and those of his comrades. Word of this sort of thing spreads quickly, and if your side has been torturing/executing prisoners, guess what is likely to happen to you if you get captured.)

Article 4 of the Geneva Convention defines prisoners of war as:

- Members of the armed forces as well as militias or volunteer units forming part of the armed forces.

- Members of other militias and other volunteer corps, including organised resistance groups operating in or outside their own territory, even if this territory is occupied, provided they fulfil the following conditions:
  1) That all be commanded by a person responsible for his subordinates
  (2) They have a fixed distinctive sign recognisable at a distance
  (3) They carry weapons openly
  (4) They conduct their operations in accordance with the laws and customs of war.

- Non-military personnel accompanying the armed forces such as journalists, building contractors, members of labour units or welfare departments – provided they have received authorisation from the armed forces they accompany and possess an approved identity card.

- Ships' crews, including masters, pilots and apprentices of the merchant marine and the crews of civil aircraft who do not benefit from more favourable treatment under any other provision of international law.

Article 13 prohibits reprisals against prisoners and requires that they be humanely treated and protected against acts of violence and intimidation. When questioned, prisoners are obliged to give 'the big four': their name, rank, serial number and date of birth. 'No physical or mental torture, nor any other forms of coercion may be inflicted on prisoners of war to secure from them information of any kind whatever. Prisoners of war who refuse to answer may not be threatened, insulted, or exposed to any unpleasant or disadvantageous treatment of any kind.' Badges of rank, medals and personal possessions may not be confiscated, and if any money is taken you must give a receipt.

Prisoners of war must be held in conditions no worse than those faced by forces of the detaining power. 'The basic daily food ration shall be sufficient in quantity, quality and variety to keep prisoners of war in good health and prevent loss of weight.' Various other provisions of the treaty decree that medical treatment be provided, sports facilities or at least room for exercise must be laid on, and religious services allowed. Officers of the detaining power will be saluted as per British custom; non-commissioned prisoners will salute commissioned officers and officers salute those officers superior to them.

TAKING PRISONERS

Surrendering is a dangerous action. Countless soldiers have met their deaths on the 'too late chum' principle: if you shoot down man after man attacking your position then meekly put up your hands when the survivors close in, they might not play by the rules. Brigadier Peter Young, who came to fame as a commando leader in World War Two, shot plenty of enemy soldiers, but always said he could never bear to kill someone not wearing a helmet. So if the game's up for you, take off your helmet and generally try to look more like a human being than another 'faceless' enemy.

However, the act of taking a prisoner can be equally dangerous for the would-be captor. Many guerrilla movements and even some regular armies have opted for suicide rather than surrender, and often a suicide that involves taking as many of the enemy with them as possible. The classic case is the wounded enemy lying on the ground, awaiting capture; you kneel down, roll him over and 'bang', the hidden grenade goes off.

Before you have to worry about any of the Geneva Convention rules, you first have to take your prisoner without falling for any of the nasty tricks and booby-traps that are possible in this situation. The first thing is to ensure that the prisoner is disarmed. It is a two-man job in which one man searches while his oppo covers the prisoner with a weapon. Make sure the covering man has a clear shot at all times in case the prisoner tries something. And always make the enemy come to you if he indicates he wishes to surrender. Don't make the mistake of leaving cover only to be shot. This was a favourite trick in World War One and happened again on the Falklands where two members of the Parachute Regiment were killed trying to accept a surrender. Once you have satisfied yourself that you have removed the prisoner's means to shoot, stab or otherwise kill you, take and tag any documents he/she is carrying except for individual ID cards.

Prisoners should be searched minutely, preferably while in a stress position against a wall. Make them lean forward, feet wide apart, taking their weight on their fingertips. This way they cannot react quickly. One man searches, while his oppo covers. Watch the prisoner's expression while you search as you might get a clue when you are getting close to something. Work systematically, starting with the helmet or hat, then the hair, jacket, shirt etc. Favourite hiding places are the armpits, the small of the back (room here for a dagger or small pistol), and the groin.

If you have taken several prisoners, make sure they are separated as soon as possible so they cannot co-ordinate a story or pass each other items of equipment. Keep private soldiers away from NCOs and segregate the officers. Remember that if they thought capture was imminent, officers/NCOs might have torn off their insignia, hoping to be taken for ordinary soldiers. So look at them carefully. And search their position – if you find a radio, there's bound to be a set of instructions. What frequency is the radio on?

Taking prisoners is a skill seldom practised properly, but like any military activity the more it is rehearsed the better it will work on the day. The opposite is equally true, so rehearse the whole routine, and have as your 'prisoners' the members of your team most proficient in unarmed combat. Then you will discover just how quickly the tables can be turned on you if you fail to take care. At best, you will discover during the debrief that you failed to find some crucial documents or kit that would have been useful to military intelligence. At worse, your 'prisoner' might escape, or even take you prisoner!

TACTICAL QUESTIONING

Armies have learned that the best time to extract any information from a prisoner is as soon as possible after capturing them. Being captured is a profoundly shocking experience that will shake even the hardest individuals. How armies do this varies from place to place and from time to time. In the Gulf War the Iraqis usually favoured an old-fashioned kicking. Primitive brutality certainly can work, but is not that effective against highly motivated soldiers. In Vietnam and South America, tactical questioning was at times performed in a helicopter with failure to answer accurately leading to the subject's ejection through the doorway 3000 feet up. But as noted above, all this sort of thing is counter-productive and guarantees that members of your own side will suffer equally gruesome treatment if they fall into enemy hands. There is another good reason too. It is undeniable that people will say anything in such a situation, anything to stop the pain or to stay alive. So you will be told what they think you want to hear, and you may never get to the truth at all.

You suspect your prisoner knows a good deal about the enemy's dispositions, strength and intentions. How, then, do you extract the information within the restrictions of the Geneva Convention? If you have several prisoners, you can give the weakest-looking ones better treatment, so it looks as if they are helping you. This can encourage others to come forward and volunteer information in the hope of getting the same. It can also make a prisoner so frightened of his fellow prisoners that he will tell all he knows to avoid being placed back with them. Boredom and isolation are two useful weapons: long periods deprived of natural light and access to a watch will disorientate the prisoner. The interrogation session can came as a welcome relief from the sheer tedium of sitting about on a cold stone floor.

Once you get past 'the big four' and they start to talk, off you go. You might get them talking about something utterly trivial at first. Informal chatting with Argentine prisoners generated a lot of information during the Falklands War, partly because of the generally low motivation among the Argentines but also because a few British officers spoke Spanish and were able to get them at their ease. Old tricks like showing off just how much you appear to know (so they think, 'Oh, no harm in talking then, these guys already know') are often successful. So make sure you have done your homework, and know as much as possible about the enemy forces. Get the prisoner to confirm something even he appreciates you already know. Get him into the frame of mind that it will do no harm if he talks, and he will be treated much better if he does.

Life is obviously much easier if you can speak the enemy's language. If you have to conduct an interrogation via an interpreter, you must take care that he or she does not end up taking control of the questioning. You will then find it hard to determine whether you are hearing what the prisoner has actually said or the interpreter's opinion of what was said. Since your interpreter might not have any military experience, this can be a big problem. The best way is to use the interpreter as a machine: you ask a question, they translate. Prisoner answers, interpreter translates. Your turn again. Alternatively, you can give the interpreter a couple of points you want answered, let them talk and receive the answers. For instance, you might want the subject's name, age and occupation. Get the answers and then give the interpreter the next set of points. But don't let them jabber away while you try to puzzle out what's going on. Stay in control.

You can also work the 'hard man/soft man' routine, with one guy working into a real frenzy, shouting, swearing and gradually going over the top. He is then thrown out by a quietly spoken, reasonable fellow who gives the prisoner a cup of tea and a cigarette and asks basically the same questions but in the opposite way. It may sound corny, but when you've had no sleep for three days, you're cold, hungry and thirsty and really don't have a clue what's going on, even the best-trained men and women can fall for such basically simple techniques.

RESISTANCE TO INTERROGATION

No video, instruction pamphlet or textbook will teach you how to stay silent under brutal interrogation. You cannot learn how to resist torture. Resistance to interrogation is taught to Western special forces by going about as far as you can without breaking the international laws outlined above. Sleep and sensory deprivation, humiliation, cold, white noise etc. can reduce even the toughest SAS volunteers to a state of gibbering incoherence. It's easy to say 'It's only an exercise' from the comfort of your bar stool, but when it's you spread-eagled against the wall in a derelict Welsh farmhouse for the second night in a row, you may sing a different tune. However, all such exercises have to be conducted carefully; moral considerations aside, there is no sense causing permanent psychological or physical injury to one of your own men. Russian, Iranian, North Korean and a few other forces are less concerned and their losses on training reflect this.

The function of Western-style resistance to interrogation is to prepare men (and, nowadays, women) for the shock of capture. The hope is that they have at least some experience of what it will be like to be captured, and that armed with the confidence that comes from having survived the course on exercise, they will be better placed to resist. But it is not just about surviving rough treatment. The real lesson to be learnt is that you have to stay alert, even when kept up night after night, in order to detect enemy trickery. Few of the tricks will be original, but they can all work on the tired and the frightened as we have mentioned above.

Suppose you have resisted the lure of the 'soft man' after the barrage of abuse from the 'hard man'. Brain reeling from lack of sleep, you've kept repeating the big four and refused to answer any other question. Disgusted, the guards dump you back in a cellar where you find a fellow prisoner. He may be injured. You talk, describe what's been happening. The fellow 'prisoner' may be a 'stool pigeon' – a prisoner who has been forced or otherwise persuaded to work for the enemy. He might be a genuine prisoner, but there might be a hidden microphone in the room, broadcasting your conversation to the enemy. He might be an enemy agent.

Keep your temper. Interrogators look for weakness and this is as likely to be over-aggressiveness as timidity. On the SAS escape and evasion exercise I mentioned when discussing patrols, the security forces realised we were all heading for the same bit of coast because of the settings on our compasses. What they didn't know was how we had planned to get away from there – by boat, helicopter, sub? So they got one of the prisoners, a big Jock, and just took the piss out of him. They said, 'What a fucking wanker, how were you going to get to the submarine anyway?' Assuming they had already tumbled that it was to be a sub picking us up, he said we wouldn't have had far to swim. One of the oldest tricks in the book, but it works.

Interrogators will search for something, building on earlier answers or something you said to a fellow prisoner or just your physical appearance. Taunting, ridicule and insulting of everything you hold sacred will follow, and it is easy to get involved in a mutual slanging match. You may find yourself inadvertently blurting out something of use to them. So whatever they say about you, your genital construction, your mother or Manchester United, stick to telling them your name, rank, number and date of birth.

Survival Skills

Interest in survival skills has snowballed over the last ten years or so. The British Army in general, and the SAS in particular, are paying greater attention than ever before to fundamental skills that enable soldiers to survive using local resources and their own knowledge. This is due in no small part to the efforts of a number of survival instructors, both military and civilian, who have popularised the idea. In countries like Canada and Sweden, where harsh winter conditions are a real risk for service personnel, survival training has always been hard and realistic. The explosion of interest in the subject has led to an amazing cross-fertilisation of ideas – comparing the winter survival skills of, say, Siberians and Inuit or the methods used to cope with daytime temperatures of over fifty degrees centigrade in Namibia and the Australian bush.

With soldiers more likely than ever to find themselves suddenly deployed to some remote troublespot, a thorough understanding of survival techniques is important. So if a transport helicopter crashes, pitching you into the middle of the African bush, you will know how to look after yourself and your team. With the knowledge comes a self-confidence that will do no harm either. But as with everything else in this book, it's no good just reading about it. You have to practise to make perfect, and there is one important point that you must take note of. From practising fire-making to searching for water or building shelters, you must leave nothing behind but your footprints. Tidy up and take your rubbish home; leave the countryside as you would wish to find it. (And there is a practical military value in this too. If you get into the habit of never leaving the least bit of rubbish in your wake, your patrols will be that much harder for anyone to track.)

WATER

You do not have to be in the desert to experience a water shortage. Water sources can be hard to find even in temperate forests, where poor visibility (and, possibly, enemy action) may hide obvious sites. The importance of water is obvious, but it is worth restating: you can do without food for days without a significant reduction in your ability, but dehydration catches up with you much, much faster.

Water flows downhill, and where there is water there is usually lush green vegetation. Animals and birds need water too, so keep a look-out for them. Listen for the croak of a frog, seldom found far from water. You can use an absorbent material to get water from dew before the morning sunshine causes it to evaporate. Brush a cloth across the vegetation and squeeze out the water into a container. Although time-consuming, this method can work very successfully, providing you remember to boil the water before drinking it. Dew is pure, but your cloth and the vegetation you're wiping it from probably are not. The same applies to rainwater, often your most reliable source of water. Water from puddles can be drunk, once purified. Water also collects in hollows in trees, ending up strongly tainted with tannin. You can exploit this: boil it, then dilute with clean water before drinking to get a little tannin inside you (useful for treating diarrhoea), or use the boiled tannin-water as an antiseptic application for wounds.

Snow is a stunningly inefficient water source: by boiling ten buckets of snow you will end up with one bucket of water. Ice is a far better source, but it is never going to be pure and you need to boil the water rather than just melt the ice.

One source to use with the greatest caution is the obvious one: rivers. In exotic parts of the world, rivers and streams often contain deadly parasites and water-borne diseases. In developed countries, agriculture is so chemically dependent that waterways are polluted with all sorts of nasties that require filtration and boiling to deal with. And then you can get really unlucky, like the SAS soldier evading through Iraq who drank from a stream that turned out to be a waste pipe from one of Saddam's nuclear facilities.

FIRE

It is possible to make fire by rubbing the proverbial two sticks together, but you need the right wood and a great deal of practice to get it right. You also need to be fit: it takes a lot of elbow grease to get the tinder to ignite and an arm injury would make it next to impossible to achieve. It remains, however, an important and useful technique, especially in desert areas where the necessary bone-dry wood can be found. Old bamboo works well too. Split a piece a couple of inches in diameter and cut a notch crossways. Place some tinder in the hollow and saw above it with the other half of the bamboo. The friction will eventually get the wood to ignition point.

If you take the time to learn a few fire-making techniques like this, you will certainly feel more confident in the field. It is better to carry your fire-making kit 'in your head' than on your belt or in your Bergen. However, a little modern hardware will save you a great deal of time and effort, so for practical reasons get to know how to start fires with flint and steel. This is nothing more than a flint rod with a bit of hacksaw blade that you scrape across the stone to produce sparks. Use fine wood shavings, scraps of bark, dry grass or ferns for tinder. If you cannot find any dry tinder where you are, scour your pockets for bits of fluff and fibre. You can also break open a field dressing to use the cotton wool padding inside. For added refinement, get a combination flint/magnesium block. Shave bits of magnesium into the tinder, which burns fiercely, making the tinder easier to ignite even when a little damp. Alternatively, pull the bullet out of a rifle or pistol round and empty the propellant into the tinder. If the situation allows it, you can always use your weapon to start the fire. Pull out the bullet, insert some cloth and chamber the round. Fire it and the cloth will be shot out, smouldering.

Even if you don't smoke, carry a Zippo lighter which will light in almost any situation. It will work on most liquid fuels, so you do not have to carry special cans of lighter fuel with you. It is certainly more reliable than the service-issue waterproof matches that come in a strip of tin foil, although these are useful too. The chunky 'lifeboat' matches that come in a waterproof container are a better bet, but do not split them into halves or quarters, as is sometimes advised. If you want lots of matches, buy some more before you go. To eke out your supply, take a tallow candle with you. Light the candle and use its flame to start your fire – it will burn more reliably and you won't waste several matches getting the fire going. Little birthday cake candles are useful for the same reason, but you can always use a tallow candle (animal fat, after all) in your cooking if the food supply is low.

British Army-issue hexamine tablets, as used on the issue stove, can be broken up and used as firelighters, but remember that the fumes are toxic so do not burn much of the stuff in a confined space. For military purposes the jellied alcohol stoves are the best, and not just for the Arctic for which they were originally developed. Because they do not smoke and do not make a smell, they can be used in observation posts near the enemy or by patrols which are trying to remain hidden.

FOOD

Since World War Two, most recruits in Western armies have come from urban backgrounds and have little or no understanding of the countryside. These days, almost everyone buys their meat pre-cut in packs from the supermarket; families no longer keep chickens, rabbits and the odd pig to eat. So not only do few young soldiers have the skills to hunt animals for food, they won't have a clue how to skin and butcher them either.

4 MARKSMANSHIP

The British Army has always prided itself on marksmanship. Accurate rapid fire by the regular soldier of the BEF (British Expeditionary Force) led the Germans to believe they were facing lines of machine guns in 1914. In fact, the British had no more machine guns than the Germans then, but because they were paid a bonus for having a marksman's badge, the British regulars had put in a lot of range time, and most of the soldiers sent to France were earning the extra money. The age of computers and smart weapons has not reduced the value of good marksmanship. The ability to shoot accurately despite the intense mental stress of a firefight remains as vital as ever, especially in counter-insurgency situations where political factors might limit the amount of fire support you can call on.

Familarity with firearms can only come from practice and experience. You can buy all the gun books you like, but they can never be a substitute for hands-on knowledge. What follows will brief you on the basics of battle shooting, but only regular practice will turn you into a competent battle shot.

Range safety

The first and most important consideration is range safety. This is drummed into recruits from day one, but it is remarkable how soon such fundamental precautions are neglected, often by people who should know better. They say familiarity breeds contempt; perhaps this is why experienced soldiers can sometimes be the worst offenders, frequent use of weapons leading to a rather cavalier attitude. Practise your load, unload and make-safe drills until they are automatic, conditioned responses. Remember that it is better to make an apparently unnecessary check than to fire a shot by mistake. More than one soldier's last words have been 'I didn't mean to do that' after shooting himself by accident while fiddling with a rifle. *Always* assume that a weapon is loaded until you have proved that it is clear.

Principles of marksmanship

Marksmanship
(a) A split group: This is usually the result of a slight change in your shooting position while firing the group. Test the natural alignment of your position before firing and do not alter the position of your elbows (especially) while firing a group.

(b) A vertical group shows you are aiming correctly in one dimension, but your eye is probably not staying in a consistent position to the sights. Keep your head still and concentrate on getting the same sight picture every time.

(c) A group appearing to the left and high of the aiming point probably means that you are not gripping the rifle correctly. The butt is coming out of your shoulder.

(d) A diagonal group crossing the aiming point like this is usually the result of you moving your head while firing the group.

(e) A good group with one 'yer' miles off target: this is often the result of failing to maintain a proper sight picture or anticipating the shot. Keep a consistent sight picture and

Whatever weapon you are issued with or acquire, the five principles of marksmanship apply:

1. Your firing position must be stable enough to support the weapon.
2. The weapon must be pointing naturally at the target.
3. Your sight alignment must be correct.
4. Your breathing must be under control and the trigger operated correctly.
5. The shot must be released and 'followed through'.

There is nothing magical about the principles of marksmanship. They are nothing more than common sense and physical reality. Most service rifles are capable of tremendous accuracy if fired from a bench rest, but under combat conditions they do not achieve anything like their theoretical best. You, the shooter, introduce all sorts of variables: ring from uncomfortable and unstable positions, not concentrating on your sights, panting like a dog because you've just sprinted a hundred metres and snatching at the trigger because you are

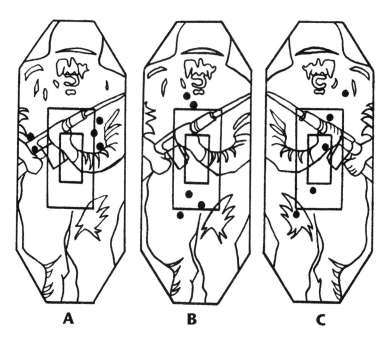

A   **B**   **C**

concentrate on trigger control and follow through.

(f) What group? A scattering of shots all over the shop means that you are not being consistent. Your firing position must remain the same, likewise your sight picture and you must `squeeze' or `press' the trigger never snatch at it.

(g) This is the sort of tight group you must be able to shoot consistently before you can zero your personal weapon. The siz of your group will be proportional to the range, so its diameter at 100 metres will be four times its diameter at 25m.

frightened. To achieve a high standard of accuracy in battle you practise shooting under the most realistic conditions you can, and you apply the principles of marksmanship until they become second nature, a set of conditioned responses that your brain will continue to make even under the most terrible stress.

The firing position must be stable because if you or the weapon is wobbling about, the bullets are likely to disperse over a wide area. Hold the weapon firmly, but not too tightly; if your posture is too tense it becomes counter-productive and harder to aim properly. For the same reason, the weapon must point naturally at the target; in other words, you are not having to apply pressure to keep it on target. You will soon see what a difference this makes on the range. Adopt a firing position, close your eyes and hold it. When you open them, you will probably find the sights are pointing some way off the target. So move your elbows or realign your whole body and repeat the procedure until, when you open your eyes, the weapon is pointing correctly.

Breathing, especially rapid breathing, causes body movement that will dramatically affect your aim. The more unfit you are, the harder it is and the longer it takes to get your breathing under sufficient control to shoot accurately, hence the importance of aerobic exercise. To fire a shot with the minimum disturbance from breathing, breathe in a regular

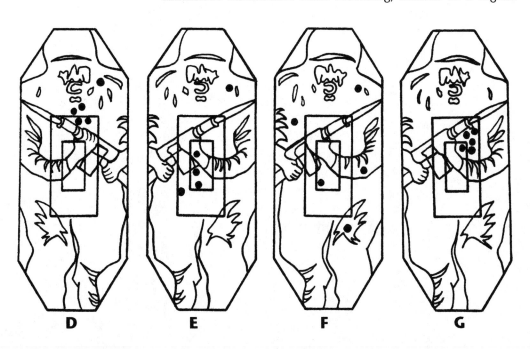

D   E   F   G

rhythm and take a couple of deep breaths once in a firing position. Breathe in, pause as you take aim, breathe out just a little and hold it. Squeeze off the shot and breathe out fully. Don't try and hold your breath too long or you will begin involuntary movement that will spoil your aim.

'Follow through' means not altering your position after you have pulled the trigger. Don't release the trigger immediately the shot is fired, hold it back and keep your eye on the fore-sight. The rifle's recoil will push the barrel upwards, but if you are in a good solid firing position and your hold is firm enough, the sights should settle back to your point of aim.

GROUPING

To zero a military rifle correctly, you need to fire half-a-dozen five-shot groups at 100 metres. Measure each group of shots – the mid-point between the extreme ends of the group is known as the MPI (Mean Point of Impact). By firing several groups, you establish an average of the MPIs which can then be compared to your POA (Point Of Aim) and the sights can be adjusted accordingly. Vertical adjustments are made by raising or lowering the foresight; lateral adjustments are made by moving the rear sight to the right or left. In the Rhodesian Army we did our grouping at twenty-five metres, working on the edge of the butts and using a one-inch patch. It just saved us walking down 100 metres to check our shots.

APPLICATION OF FIRE

On a firing range you usually know the exact range of the targets, but in combat you have to work it out for yourself. And in the excitement of battle, soldiers often forget to change the settings on their sights. If your sights are set for the wrong range, you are unlikely to hit anything. Learning to judge ranges is something that only comes with experience. Ranges of objects are often over-estimated when

- kneeling or lying
- an object is only partly visible
- looking across broken ground
- looking over a valley or undulating ground
- looking down avenues, long streets or ravines

- the object is in the shade
- it is misty or in bad light
- heat is rising from the ground
- the background is the same colour as the object.

Ranges are often under-estimated when

- the sun is behind you
- you are in bright sunshine or very clear weather conditions
- when the background and the object are different colours
- you are looking over level ground
- you are looking over snow or water
- you are looking up or down

At ranges over 100 metres, a strong crosswind will push a bullet 'off course'. This is more noticeable with 5.56mm rifles or Soviet 7.62 _ 39mm weapons than with something firing 7.62 _ 51mm NATO ammunition. Again, this is something that can only come with practice, but if you keep a log of sessions on the range, noting the different conditions, you will soon discover just how much you need to 'aim off' to counteract the effect of the wind.

FIRING POSITIONS

Lying prone is the most stable position and the one that will deliver the greatest accuracy. However, you will often discover that long grass or other vegetation blocks your line of sight if you lie on the deck. You will often have to fire from kneeling, squatting, sitting or standing positions, so you must practise firing from these positions until it is second nature.

Standing

Stand with your feet about a shoulder width apart, in line with the target. The left elbow should be directly underneath the rifle, the left hand cradling rather than tightly griping the weapon. The butt is positioned high against your shoulder, with the right arm kept horizontal. Turn very slightly to the right and lean slightly forwards in the direction of the target. The weight of the rifle and the inevitable movement caused by recoil makes this a difficult posture to sustain for any length of time, so relax into the alert position when you are not actually firing.

Kneeling

Face half right to the target and kneel on your right knee, sitting (if possible) on the heel or side of your foot. Now turn the left foot inwards to steady your left leg and reduce movement. Your weight should be resting mainly on your right heel. Keep the rifle butt high on your shoulder.

Sitting

This is a good option when firing through low vegetation or from a hillside. It is probably the best position from which to engage moving targets and is a favourite for ambushing because you can remain in position without the discomfort of other postures. Sit with your legs apart or crossed (whichever you find more comfortable) with the rifle held in the same way as in the kneeling position, except that your elbows should be in front of, or resting on the top of, your knees.

Squatting

If you are in shallow water, mud or other terrain which makes other firing positions difficult, this is the best bet. However, 'rice paddy prone', as it's known, is uncomfortable to maintain and few non-oriental soldiers can manage it for long. Plant your feet a shoulder's width apart and drop down onto your haunches in a natural squatting position. The backs of your thighs should be resting on the backs of your calves with the knees bent to their fullest extent. Your weight should be evenly divided between the balls of your feet.

On the move

When moving through woods, jungle or other close country, patrolling grey or patrolling green, you have to be ready to shoot back immediately. The enemy may have seen you first and you could be attacked without warning. But if you can return fire instantly, and accurately, you can turn the tables on them. The following are the standard methods of carrying a rifle:

The alert position

Keep the left hand on the hand guard and the right on the pistol grip. The butt of the weapon is positioned low on your shoulder with the muzzle pointing down at about forty-five degrees. Although your trigger finger is (obviously) outside the trigger guard, fingertip touching the receiver, the safety is off, so take care not to muzzle sweep anyone you don't plan on shooting. Apply the safety when crossing obstacles.

Cradle carry

This is similar, but comes from the British Army's experience of hanging around Belfast street corners wearing body armour. Hold the rifle as in the alert position but with the butt resting on the outside of your right arm rather than low on the shoulder. The weight of the weapon is taken on the elbow.

High Port

This is used for advancing to contact through low cover. The rifle is carried in a diagonal hold across the body with your left hand on the rifle guard and your right on the pistol grip and the barrel pointing upwards. The safety is off and the trigger finger rests on the trigger, so take care and apply the safety when crossing obstacles. The idea of this position is that you are ready to fire, but if you fall over the weapon you will not get tangled up in the vegetation or get dirt into the muzzle.

Low Port

This is used when you need one hand free for searching suspects, checking documents etc. in an internal security situation. Hold the pistol grip with your right hand, finger outside the trigger guard and safety applied. The barrel points upwards with the butt resting on your hip or waist belt.

Shooting from cover

The expression 'eye for ground' is widely used in military histories, usually with reference to generals who saw a way to exploit the lie of the land to win a battle. The same idea works for the individual rifleman. Although he may have less scope for choosing where to fight, the soldier who makes best use of the ground will often win the firefight. Slight folds in the ground can offer protection for most of your body, but it takes a bit of experience to take in the possibilities of a set piece of ground quickly enough to make the best of them in combat. A good fire position gives you some protection from direct fire from enemy small arms and high explosives, but also offers a wide arc of fire with nothing blocking the view.

When shooting from cover you should rest your forearm to

support the rifle. At least use the cover to support the back of your hand or rest the weapon itself on something, although you should not rest only the barrel which would affect its resonance and move the MPI. Don't assume you have to fire *over* cover; if it is at all possible, fire *through* cover. A ring position behind a loophole in a wall is far harder for the enemy to spot than your head and rifle leaning over the top of it.

Pay attention to muzzle clearance when firing over folds in the ground. If your muzzle is too low to the ground, the propellant gases will kick up a lot of dust, betraying your position.

Concealment

Don't confuse 'cover from fire' with 'cover from view' by sheltering behind something that is not actually bulletproof. Breezeblocks and single-brick walls provide little protection against rifle bullets and none at all against machine gun fire. If you are occupying a position among low vegetation for any period of time, you will probably find a sitting position most effective. It is reasonably comfortable and enables you to engage targets over a wide arc without shifting posture.

Battle shooting

There are three basic types of rifle fire used in combat: deliberate shooting, snap shooting and rapid fire.

DELIBERATE SHOOTING

Deliberate fire comprises carefully aimed single shots used primarily against targets at longer ranges. This calls for rigorous attention to the principles of marksmanship discussed above. Unless there is a pressing reason to do so, you should be firing no more than half-a-dozen shots in a minute.

SNAP SHOOTING

Snap shooting comprises single shots or 'double taps' (two shots in quick succession) at targets that are briefly visible, and is rather faster. You will usually be moving, in the alert position, looking for the enemy. As soon as a target appears, restrain your breathing, aim and fire. Take care not to snatch the trigger but pull it correctly and follow through. Keep shooting until the target falls or goes behind cover. If the target does not go down, get yourself into cover and carry on from there. You have to accept that the need to get off a round as quickly as possible will prevent you thinking your way through the principles of marksmanship. So make sure your stance is balanced and stable at all times and concentrate on your sight alignment. Be careful if you are using optical sights, which tend to make you focus through them, narrowing your field of vision.

RAPID FIRE

Rapid fire comprises strings of shots usually fired at clearly definable targets at short range. Twenty aimed rounds a minute is rapid fire; too rapid to think through every single round, but not so fast you cannot get into a rhythm with your breathing and shoot properly in a co-ordinated manner. With each shot, you should be able to restrain your breath and get a good sight picture before squeezing the trigger. If you can manage it, hold your breath as per deliberate shooting but fire two rounds before breathing normally. But remember that your aim will suffer if you try to hold your breath and sight picture for more than seven or eight seconds. Rapid fire heats up rifles to an uncomfortable degree, so if you get a pause in the firing, lock back the action to allow air to circulate around the chamber.

FULL AUTO

Fully automatic fire from an assault rifle is incredibly inaccurate even at very short ranges. There are few situations in which you are better advised to fire full auto than to stick to rapid (but aimed) single shots. Not only is fully automatic fire inaccurate, it eats up your ammo at an incredible rate. There is no real consensus here: the British Army stuck with a semi-automatic weapon for years (the SLR or L1A1) until adopting the L85; many armies have rifles capable of firing three-round bursts rather than sustained automatic fire; some rifles offer you a choice between full auto and burst fire. The US Army has converted its M16s from full auto to three-round bursts, concluding that the full auto facility just led to soldiers emptying their rifles to no real effect. African guerrillas tended to fire fully automatic the whole time, and most of it went straight over our heads. You had more chance of being hit by a fluke than of someone actually aiming at you.

MOVING TARGETS

A target moving across your line of sight might travel far or fast enough to be out of the way when your bullet arrives. So, depending on the range, direction and the speed of the target's movement, you will have to aim off to compensate for this. Aiming to anticipate a target's movement is called 'lead'. There are two schools of thought here, and only regular practice will determine which works best for you. The basic method is to aim behind the target and swing the rifle round until the sights are on the target's leading edge. Fire a succession of shots, increasing the amount of lead if necessary. Alternatively, aim at a point in front of the target and start firing just before the target reaches it. Keep firing so the target effectively moves into the path of the bullets.

RIFLE STOPPAGES

Most military rifles are designed for combat conditions rather than the cosseted life of a target rifle. Yet even the most robust combat rifle needs some care and maintenance if it is to go bang when you need it to. Before we look at the IAs (Immediate Actions) that must become second nature to deal with stoppages, I should stress that it is better to avoid stoppages by having a well-maintained rifle than to find yourself racking the slide and reseating the magazine halfway through a firefight.

Before looking at the various mechanical problems that can jam a rifle, there is one point that should be taken to heart. The most common cause of a 'stoppage' is that you have an empty magazine. Count your rounds. Put a couple of tracer rounds at the bottom of each magazine and change mags before each new phase of the operation.

Keep all metal surfaces of your rifle clean using a suitable nitro solvent. Strip down the bolt carrier group and clean it regularly, and if you are using a rifle designed like the M16 (where the gas bleeds directly on to the bolt) clean out the inside of the carrier key. The extractor, extractor well and bolt-locking lugs must be clear of carbon deposits. Use solvent on a patch to clean the inside of the receiver. Old toothbrushes and pipe cleaners get into odd corners and are useful for cleaning the trigger group. Use plenty of solvent and a brush to clean the bore and chamber, then swab out the barrel with clean patches until they pass through clean. Clean the gas system too, removing all deposits of fouling. Give the bore a very light oiling if the weapon is going into storage for any length of time.

The bore, chamber, firing pin and all external surfaces require a light coat of gun oil. You can be generous on the outside of the bolt carrier and the inside of the receiver. Don't forget to check your magazines too. Take them apart regularly and clean them out; put a little oil on the follower spring but nowhere else. Ditch any magazines with damaged lips or major dents in them.

Accidental discharges happen, and they sometimes have tragic consequences. However, there was one incident in Africa which still led to a result for us, although if the guy hadn't fired when he did, we might have done better. I was leading a Pathfinder patrol, scouting ahead of a regular SADF infantry company. Just as we came over a hill I saw this guy's hat move, although it was barely visible under the shade of a big tree. If we'd been bimbling along with the rest of the company, I'd never have spotted the enemy because he would have seen and heard us first. As it was, I said to Sean Wyatt, 'There's a guy just under that tree. If anything happens, put a blooper (40mm grenade launcher) round in there straight away.'

I got on the radio at once and brought the company up. I said, 'Right, send a section forward.' I'm manoeuvring this section into position when someone has an AD. Sean just went 'whump' and got the guy right in the chest! Of course, the rest of the company rushes the place and the guy was shot 116 times – he was like a colander by the time they were firnished with him. There had been five enemy there; we picked up five packs. But the guy we killed was the second-in-command of SWAPO. The amount of intelligence we got from that kill was phenomenal.

SUB-MACHINE GUNS

The sub-machine gun was dismissed as a 'gangster weapon' by most armies when it first came out, and it took World War Two to prove how useful a weapon it was. The image lives on to this day, however: year after year we are treated to new action movies in which people hose their enemies with SMGs, firing from the hip. It doesn't work like that in real life.

To shoot accurately with a sub-machine gun, you need to apply all the principles of marksmanship, especially the first. You have to assume a firing position which provides the maximum stability. SMGs fire pistol cartridges and have a much shorter sight base than a rifle. Many sub-machine guns fire from an open bolt, which compounds these shortcomings, the movement of the heavy bolt back and forth making precise shooting impossible. Others, most famously the Heckler and Koch MP5 (popularised by the SAS in the Iranian Embassy assault and very widely used by US law enforcement teams), fire from a closed bolt. This is enormously better and enables you to shoot with real accuracy.

The point of aim of a high-velocity rifle does not vary significantly up to 300 metres, but sub-machine guns are very different. You have to aim off to compensate for the ballistic properties of the 9mm Parabellum round fired by most SMGs.

MARKSMANSHIP

Zero the weapon at twenty-five metres, firing from a stable kneeling position. Start by firing single shots into a Figure 11 target from twenty-five metres. You need to achieve a six-inch (150mm) group with five rounds. Once you can do so with consistency, zero the weapon so that it fires to the point of aim at twenty-five metres. Then fire test groups at fifty, seventy-five and a hundred metres and note how much you will have to aim off as the target gets further away. The MPI will also vary according to whether you are standing, kneeling or lying down.

Squeezing off accurate single shots with an open-bolt submachine gun takes a bit of practice, which is the main reason that Western armies have pretty well abandoned this type of weapon. Squeezing the trigger releases the sear, allowing the bolt to fly forward, strip the top round out of the magazine, chamber and fire it. All this internal movement tends to upset your aim, so you have to concentrate. Squeeze the trigger carefully and follow through.

The classic assault position – shooting from the hip – can work with an SMG. Indeed, within ten metres or so it is the best option since you won't have time to squint along the sights. Because you are not aiming the weapon properly when firing from the underarm assault position, you must make doubly sure you have a stable firing position. Keep your balance. Fire a series of very short bursts, just two or three rounds each rather than one long burst. Pull the trigger and release it smartly. Short bursts are easier to control and you can effectively 'walk' them on to the target. A thirty-round magazine should give you ten such short bursts, but it is better to change magazines after five or six bursts to give some margin for error. So learn to count them as you go. And when you do need to change magazines, do not just drop them on the ground – you will need them again – but get into cover and then do the mag change. The same applies to clearing stoppages, which should be an instinctive drill carried out under cover.

PISTOLS

It takes a reasonable degree of skill to hit a man-sized target at fifty metres with a pistol. So to the British Army, pistols have been either a token weapon issued to officers, signallers or other specialists who do not carry rifles, or back-up weapons for hostage rescue teams or undercover work in internal security operations. The relative ineffectiveness of the pistol as a military weapon has led to a general lack of interest in its development. The British Army has used the same pre-war Browning pistol design for the last fifty years; the US Army's Colt .45 pistol entered service in 1911 and was only retired in the late 1980s. Many armies today are still using the same handguns they had in the 1950s. Not just old designs – old guns. Many of the Brownings recently retired from the British Army were shot out and fit only to be melted down.

Armies' lack of interest in the pistol extends to training too. Although many soldiers are issued with them, there is little time allocated to training. And since pistols are harder to learn to shoot accurately than either rifles or SMGs, a generally low standard of pistol handling results. This can have tragic consequences. The two British Army signallers murdered by a mob in Northern Ireland a few years ago had a Browning 9mm pistol but were apparently unfamiliar with its operation, especially its inability to fire if the magazine is not properly housed. Weapon handling is not just about hitting the target, it is about how to clear stoppages and get the weapon back into action as quickly as possible. It is difficult to avoid the conclusion that had those men been taught to use a pistol properly, rather than just signing one out as a matter of routine, they may have survived the incident.

If you are operating as part of a mercenary unit or in a specialist troop that can select its own hardware, you will probably be able to obtain a pistol as a back-up weapon. But the weapon is only of value if you know how to use it, so zero the thing and get to know its characteristics before you have to draw it in anger. Pistols have short barrels and hence a short sight radius, so every aiming error you make will be magnified.

One reason armies dislike pistols is that, next to grenade training, teaching recruits to shoot pistols can be dangerous for pupils and instructors alike. Pistols are so small and handy, it is very easy to muzzle sweep other people on the firing range. Add unfamiliar safety devices and terrible pistol handling techniques routinely seen on TV shows (often imitated by the inexperienced) and you have an accident waiting to happen. One common habit is for people to use the Starsky and Hutch technique (seen in most subsequent cop shows) of pointing the pistol at the sky, levelling the barrel only when ready to shoot. This is dangerous because if you press the trigger while pointing the pistol skywards there is simply no telling where the round will come down, and people have been injured *over a mile away* by such foolishness on police training areas in the UK. It is also dangerous in the sense that if you ever have to use a pistol for real, having your weapon ready to engage aircraft is not the brightest way to begin a shoot-out with enemy ground troops. Every fraction of a second counts in close-quarter battle, and there is no prize for coming second in a gunfight. Wasting time levelling the pistol might cost you your life.

The basic rules of pistol handling are the same as with any other firearm. Whenever you are handed a firearm, or hand one to someone else, *assume it is loaded* and no safety is applied. Inspect the weapon and make sure it is safe. On a firing range, any pistol out of its holster should have the slide racked back and the magazine removed, so it is obviously safe. Revolvers should have their cylinders open and all cartridges removed. Weapons should be pointed down range at all times.

Choosing your pistol

In Rhodesia the issue pistol was usually a Star automatic – not the world's greatest handgun. Many members of the Rhodesian Army therefore required their own pistols and these ranged from practical, reliable automatics to Dirty Harry-style Magnum revolvers. If you have the luxury of choosing your own handgun, the only sensible advice I can give is to select something you can hit the target with. There are people with arms like tractors who can keep a .44 Magnum on target at twenty-five metres. But if you are not one of them, there is no sense carrying a massive (and heavy) revolver about the place. A hit with anything – even a lowly .22 bullet – is infinitely better than a miss with 'the most powerful handgun in the world'. Similarly, you need something reliable, something that will fire when you need it to. Many of the most accurate pistols, designed and modified for the rarefied world of competition pistol shooting, might be deadly accurate on the range but won't stand up to the battering of hard service. Some are also fussy about ammunition quality. You need a weapon that will function acceptably on older or cheap eastern European 9mm rather than requiring match-grade brass.

Stance and grip

Until you can consistently shoot a tight group, do not bother with rapid fire. Whatever weapon you have ended up with, the first thing to do is to zero it by firing carefully-shot groups. Get the group right first – you should be able to achieve a four-inch/100mm group at twenty metres – then adjust the sights so that the group appears where the weapon is actually sighted.

One-handed pistol shooting is for John Wayne, or really dire emergencies. Normally you should shoot two-handed, in whichever position suits you the best. The so-called 'isosceles stance' is a common police technique: standing square on to the target, holding the pistol with both your controlling arm and supporting arm out straight in front of you. This is a fine, stable position, but is not the best for rapid fire and does offer the enemy the best target. The usual alternative is the 'Weaver stance', developed by Los Angeles County Sheriff Jack Weaver. For a right-handed shooter, this involves pointing your left side shoulder towards the target and keeping your feet about a shoulders width apart. Keeping your right arm straight or very slightly bent, bring the weapon into the aim with your left arm and elbow at an angle of rather more than forty-five degrees. Your right hand is cradled in the left, and pressure with the left hand onto the fingers of your right hand helps reduce the muzzle jump caused by the pistol's recoil. When firing a semi-automatic pistol you can also place the forefinger of the left hand in front of the trigger guard to give extra support. Many pistols of recent manufacture have squared-off trigger guards for exactly this purpose.

Poor trigger control is one of the most common reasons for inaccurate pistol shooting. The trigger must be squeezed positively, not snatched at. Use the pad of your trigger finger, not the joint – unless you are shooting a double-action revolver with a relatively stiff trigger pull. The pad is easier to control. Think of it as pushing a button rather than pulling a trigger.

Many modern semi-automatic pistols can be fired single or double action. Single action means that the hammer must be cocked before firing – this is either done by manually pulling it back or by the action of firing the previous shot (as on most semi-automatics produced before the 1980s). In double action firing, the action of pulling the trigger first cocks and then releases the hammer, so it tends to require a stronger pull. The advantage of a double action pistol is that it can be kept holstered with no safety applied, as the trigger pull is sufficiently stiff to prevent it going off accidentally. And it can be drawn and fired without the user having to disengage a safety catch. Well, that's the theory, and more than a few law enforcement types have blown holes in their legs, car dashboards or even airline seats as a result. There is another disadvantage: because it requires a harder pull of the trigger, the first (double action) shot will seldom group with subsequent shots fired single action. In battle you might not have the luxury of wasting your first round.

Single action pistols, like the classic Browning or Colt 1911, can be carried 'cocked and locked' (round chambered, hammer cocked but safety applied) and can be drawn and fired by someone who knows what he/she is doing without any significant delay. However, it leaves the weapon more open to dirt, and if the catch is accidentally disengaged the trigger needs just a little tap to fire. Small wonder that pistol shooters are divided into those who have had an AD (Accidental Discharge) and those who are going to have one.

Pistol stoppages

Whether it's dirt, poor ammunition or just bad luck, you might find your pistol 'jamming' at the worst possible moment. This is where practice pays off; an experienced shot can clear the stoppage and get the gun firing in less time than it takes to read this sentence. Someone who just signs out the pistol and fires a few qualifying rounds a month may not have long enough to figure out what to do in an emergency.

- If the pistol fails to fire when the hammer falls, this often means that the magazine is not seated properly and the round has not been chambered. Tap the bottom of the magazine to ensure it is seated, then pull back the slide and release it to load a new cartridge. Then fire again.

- Semi-automatics often fail to eject the spent case properly. This is known as 'stove piping' and it leaves you with a case stuck in the ejection port, jamming the slide. Grasp the slide with your weak hand so your index finger is touching the case. Then push the slide firmly to the rear, throwing the case out. Allow it to come forward, chamber a fresh round and fire again.

- In semi-automatics, the round sometimes fails to chamber properly. The slide will not close fully. This problem is resolved by pulling the slide back just a little and releasing it. If this does not work, eject the magazine and cycle the action vigorously to get rid of the duff round. Then reload and carry on.

BATTLE INOCULATION

You can train a man to be a marvellous shot, but unless he can use those skills under fire he won't be effective in battle. Battle inoculation is the term for getting men used to the noise and distraction of incoming rounds, the cackle of the AK, the crack and thump of high-velocity rounds going overhead. It teaches you how to distinguish effective enemy fire – fire that could or is causing you casualties – from other incoming.

I took an expert rifle shot in Rhodesia who had criticised the marksmanship of some of our guys and said, 'Go down to 400 metres, fire ten rounds; run to 300, fire ten rounds; run to 200 metres, fire another ten rounds, fix your bayonet and every time after I say "Up", fire two rounds at the target.' As soon as he started, I opened fire with an AK, shooting up the ground around him. He began to hurry his shots. He raced down to 200 and as he fixed his bayonet, I was putting rounds all over the bank next to him. He was knackered. Still firing, but not to the accuracy he was capable of on the range normally. He said, 'Peter, point taken.'

Battle inoculation teaches you to recognise whether fire is effective. By definition, the rounds whizzing over your head aimed by your instructor will not actually hit you. But the first time you do it, you will be frightened. Do it repeatedly, and you become comfortable with fire. I'm not saying battle inoculation will make you fearless, but it will enable you to distinguish between effective and ineffective fire. You've got to recognise that it is fear that motivates you, gets you to do certain things.

I used to take the Pathfinders down range towards live mortar fire, and on the thirteenth bomb I'd shout 'Smoke!' The whole group would advance towards the danger area (I had it carefully paced out) with shrapnel whizzing over our heads. The next thing you knew, the machine guns opened up (over our heads) while the mortars, though firing smoke now, still provided the bangs.